Clifford Odets:
HUMANE DRAMATIST

MICHAEL J. MENDELSOHN

WITH AN INTRODUCTION
BY MORRIS FREEDMAN

EVERETT / EDWARDS, inc.

133 SOUTH PECAN AVENUE
DELAND, FLORIDA 32720

Manufactured in the United States
of America, by The E. O. Painter Printing Co.,
DeLand, Florida.

For My Three Girls

"Love people, do good, help the lost and fallen, make the world happy, if you can!"

LT. COLONEL MICHAEL J. MENDELSOHN *is*
Assistant Dean for Graduate Programs and an
Associate Professor of English at the United
States Air Force Academy. He grew up in
Pittsburgh where he received his education in
the public schools and later at the University
of Pittsburgh (B.A., 1951).
Since earning his commission in the United
States Air Force in 1952, he has served in various
educational assignments in Texas, Okinawa,
and—since 1958—as a member of the English
faculty at the new United States Air Force
Academy.
While stationed in San Antonio, he received
his M.A. at Trinity University and later, upon
his return from overseas, he attended the
University of Colorado where he received a
Ph.D. in 1962.
Colonel Mendelsohn has taught English and
American literature part time for the University
of California, the University of Maryland, and
the University of Colorado. He has published
a number of articles in such periodicals as
MODERN DRAMA, THEATRE ARTS, *and* THE SHAW
REVIEW. *He has also spoken on modern drama*
topics at scholarly meetings and at the NDEA
Institute at Purdue University.
During the 1966-67 academic year, Colonel
Mendelsohn was one of forty university teachers
selected nationally by the American Council on
Education for its post-doctoral fellowship, the
Internship in Academic Administration. In this
internship, he spent the year at the Massachu-
setts Institute of Technology.

Contents

DEDICATION iii

ABOUT THE AUTHOR v

PREFACE ix

INTRODUCTION BY MORRIS FREEDMAN xiii

I. THE BACKGROUND 1

II. THE EARLY PLAYS: WRITTEN IN ANGER . . 21

III. THE MIDDLE PLAYS: IN MODERATION . . . 43

IV. THE POST-WAR PLAYS: IN MATURITY . . . 65

V. THE DRAMATIST IN HOLLYWOOD 83

VI. STYLE AND INFLUENCES 99

VII. THEMES AND CONCEPTS 111

VIII. IN FINAL APPRAISAL 127

BIBLIOGRAPHY 131

INDEX 137

Preface

$\mathcal{C}$LIFFORD ODETS DIED on August 14, 1963 at the age of 57.

Most people who knew the work of Odets thought of him as much older. He was associated with an era long past, an era of seemingly hopeless economic struggle, of idealistic aspirations, of left wing political ferment. The obituary notices reflected the fact that Odets never shook off the label which attached to him early, that of angry young man. But Odets was never very convincing as a militant leftist, even in *Waiting for Lefty*, and the evolution of his plays reveals a fairly typical movement for an American born in the first decade of this century, a movement from militancy to moderation.

Odets was always a controversial figure in American drama. From his earliest produced play, *Waiting for Lefty* in 1935, to his last, *The Flowering Peach* in 1954, Odets provoked intense reactions in his readers and viewers. Yet information on Odets' life and especially discussions of his later plays and his Hollywood work remain sparse and scattered, consisting principally of brief newspaper articles and reviews. At the end of 1962, Twayne's United States Authors Series published the first full-length study of Odets, written by R. Baird Shuman. Edward Murray's excellent study last year concentrates on eight of the plays and emphasizes structure. Professor Murray stresses, much as I do, that blindly categorizing Odets as a militant proletarian writer is a rather foolish oversimplification. Presently Dr. Margaret Brenman Gibson, a good friend of Clifford Odets in his later years, is working on a full scale and definitive biographical study. For the moment, however, Harold Clurman's *The Fervent Years* remains by far the best discussion of Odets' pre-war days as actor and writer with the Group Theatre. Clurman and others have provided the insights necessary to the understanding of the playwright as a young man; the plays speak for themselves.

During the last year of his life, there was a sudden eruption of publicity pertaining to Odets' final work as editor-in-chief for a television series, just as, from time to time, there was news of Odets the screen writer, Odets the director, Odets with a new play in preparation. Nevertheless, Odets is likely to be remembered principally for three or four of his well known plays all written when he was young.

Odets was a humanitarian by inclination and a radical by accident. He happened onto the scene and came to maturity at a moment in American drama when certain audiences and critics demanded messages with their plays, significance with their literature. But Odets was not content to remain in the "social protest" pigeonhole. He was a skilled craftsman with a style of his own which influenced a number of other playwrights. More than this, he towered above his protesting contemporaries because of his idealism, his optimism, and his faith in America. Danny Kaye, delivering the eulogy (written by Clurman) at Odets' funeral aptly stressed the playwright's humanitarian side:

> The warmth which emanated from Clifford's person was not the fire of the fanatic but the comforting, healing glow of the lover. Clifford loved. In all his plays as in all per-

sonal contacts, expressions of anger or scorn always gave way to — were indeed overwhelmed by — the passionate urge of love. His love was not abstract, not a response to a religious or philosophic injunction or commitment. It was a movement of his whole being — spirit and flesh consummated in tender gestures — direct, personal, immediate, palpable. He was constantly offering gifts. No matter how lavish they were, they were but small tokens of his desire to give the greatest gift — all of himself. No one could long be angry with such a man. He overcame our reserves, he melted all coldness.

In any full-length appraisal of Odets' work, it is the humaneness, not the radicalism, that must emerge as the dominant quality.

I would like to express grateful appreciation to Mr. William Gibson and Dr. Margaret Brenman Gibson, both of whom have been consistently gracious and helpful over several years of correspondence and discussions on Odets.

A number of colleagues of the teaching profession—particularly Professors R. B. Shuman of Duke, Jack Crouch of the University of Colorado, Stanley Weintraub of Pennsylvania State, Walter Meserve of Indiana University, Morris Freedman and Robert Shedd of the University of Maryland—have been instrumental in sustaining my interest in Odets over the years.

Of my colleagues on the faculty of the United States Air Force Academy, I would like particularly to single out for thanks Professors Peter R. Moody, Cortland Auser, and Jesse C. Gatlin, Jr. As successive heads of the English Department these officer scholars have consistently encouraged scholarly achievement at every turn of the road. More important, their approach to literature has kept the climate sunny for both students and faculty members in the English Department at the Academy.

The Academy Library staff has been unfailingly helpful in securing materials upon request.

xii

Portions of this book have appeared in modified form in *Literature and Society*, a collection of essays published by the University of Nebraska Press (1964), as well as in the following periodicals: *Modern Drama, Drama Survey, Theatre Arts,* and *Drama Critique*.

[Note: Rights in the plays of Clifford Odets (except the three mentioned below) have reverted to the Odets estate, which is represented by Harold Freedman, Brandt & Brandt, 101 Park Avenue, New York 10017. Inquiries should be directed to Brandt & Brandt.]

I gratefully acknowledge permission to use excerpts from the following works: Random House, Inc., which holds the copyrights for Odets' *Paradise Lost* (in *Six Plays of Clifford Odets*) and *The Big Knife* (1949), as well as the excerpt from the Preface to *Six Plays of Clifford Odets*, 1939; Viking Press, Inc., for the excerpt from Odets' *The Country Girl*, copyright 1951; and Alfred A. Knopf, Inc., for the passages from Harold Clurman's *The Fervent Years*, copyright 1945. (Pagination in this book is from the later paperback edition, Hill and Wang, Inc., 1957, by arrangement with Alfred A. Knopf, Inc.)

Finally, I cannot neglect to comment on the kindness of Clifford Odets himself. Over the years he most graciously answered letters, discussed other matters by telephone, and most considerately invited me into his home for a lengthy talk. Like his close friends who have written about him, I easily perceived in Odets a warmth, an intelligence, and an approach to life that were remarkable in all ways. His strength and vitality shone through every phrase. He left his children a proud legacy, and he left me an indelible memory of an afternoon in 1961 that will always remain one of the highlights of my life.

MJM

Introduction

Clifford Odets was the first in a line of emerging American Jewish writers of importance, including Arthur Miller, Bernard Malamud, Saul Bellow, and Philip Roth. He was, moreover, the first dramatist to use the American Jewish experience of assimilating to the Depression economy in a significant enough way to achieve a body of work placing him unmistakably in the mainstream of American drama. Before Odets, the image of the Jew in American drama was either that of the vaudeville comic, some form of caricature, as in *Abie's Irish Rose*, or of a minor, senti- mentalized background character, like the Jewish student in *Street Scene*. Odets addressed himself to the total Jewish experience, concentrating on the heart of the matter, the Jewish family and its dominant matriarch, much as O'Neill did throughout his career in working with the Irish family.

Odets was more than a theatrical pioneer only. His body of work constituted the first extended statement in depth about the Jewish experience in America generally. The novels and autobiographical accounts which were to emerge in the decades of the 40's, 50's, and 60's, in the work of Bellow, Kazin, Podhoretz, Roth, Malamud, and others, had as background the basic materials to be found in Odets. The plays and scenarios of Arthur Miller and Paddy Chayefsky surely found audiences more ready for their subject matter and dialogue as the result of Odets's pioneering. It is as a figure in the theater and in dramatic literature, however, that Odets has his preeminent place.

For all of his dramatic innovativeness and sociological insight, Odets did not begin his career in terms of "research," or from any pietistic need to make a record, or impelled by the simple political zeal of a party activist. He began his career like other great playwrights before him, Shakespeare and Ibsen, for example, as a journeyman in the theater. He felt it a form of climax to his career to become a director. He worked in the other dramatic media of our time, films and television. He worked on other subjects than the Jewish immigrant experience in New York in the 30's and 40's. He was a thoroughly professional man of the theater, not committed to a program, not simply mining his own experience as a way of finding or justifying himself, although, of course, he never felt the need to strain for any special modesty or detachment in evaluating his work. He thought himself an important person in the theater, an artist of the first order, impatiently denying "influences" of other playwrights although readily acknowledging affinities and parallels, as with Chekhov.

Odets was careful to insist that the experience of the Berger family in *Awake and Sing* was not his own experience. The biographical data support him in terms of the sheer facts, which, as so often, are beside the point. Certainly, the ear he brought to recording the idiom and rhythms, the substance, the lurking depths of communication below sheer words, all these come from an awareness of the social scene that could not have been contrived or assumed. Odets recorded the experience he lived, one way or another, one place or another. That experience may indeed not have resembled in fine detail the daily events in The Bronx of his heroes and heroines. But he did catch the intensity, however obliquely, the passionate spirit of a group of artists, actors, writers, intellectuals of various sorts, caught up in one of those periods in human history where public events force men to make their own private values, to find their own goals, to commit themselves to community enterprises that give one identity and provide one with a small area of meaning. His awareness of theatrical environment, with its articulately self-conscious and incessant self-expression, was carried over well to the highly verbal world of his striving families. The American economic depression of the 1930's, like the great famines and disasters of history, natural or man made, created a crucible in which forms of art were shaped not only as means for dealing with this specific and enormous enveloping event but also for dealing with oneself, for mapping out territories which had inner integrity and coherence without regard to large political generalizing.

The Group Theater, of which Odets found himself an integral part, although for a while a minor one, differed from those other community enterprises of the 30's, the Federal Theater Project or the Federal Writers Project, in being self-generated. The hopeful writers and directors and actors shared a vague area of political leftism, but, as one reads Mr. Mendelsohn's book and recalls the accounts in Harold Clurman's *The Fervent Years,* it becomes clear that the highly personal and professional character of the camaraderie became the dominant mode. The Group Theater never was a simple propaganda apparatus like similar communal enterprises, *The New Masses,* for example. The arguments that swirled about Odets having to do with the use of art as a weapon in the revolution no doubt were absorbed by him, but, even if he does protest so much about his freedom of thought and action as to make us suspicious, these clearly did not affect the character of his art to the point that the resulting work sank into oblivion, weighted down by the lead of momentary ideology. Where are the John Wexleys and the John Howard Lawsons who wrote at the same time as Clifford Odets?

Odets's art, his capacity for creating a setting which convinces us of its authenticity, a dialogue which catches us up with the intensity and pertinence of its conflicts, a humor that is so intertwined with the activity of the persons involved that we rarely see it as the source of quotable gags, begin to explain the continuing validity of his achievement. His text has the density and permanence of poetry. Robert Warshow brilliantly characterized him as "the poet of the Jewish middle class." The Berger family lives in the Depression; its hope for escape, Ralph, commits himself to an idealized future, based on vague revolutionary expectations. As in Sean O'Casey's *Juno and the Paycock*, we see in *Awake and Sing* more than the effect of external economic pressures on a family: we see the very dynamic structure of a family itself revealing its innermost character under the strains of outside forces. In short, it is not the revolution which engages our attention ultimately in O'-Casey or Odets, it is the nature of family life itself.

Ralph will fully awake and sing, we are led to conclude, when he is able to extricate himself from the limits imposed more by Mrs. Berger, his mother, than by the Depression, that collection of external and remote gods. We may expect that Ralph will be driven to those forms of American success that will deny and negate the constriction of his tenement origins. Odets, too, became the golden boy of the American dramatic scene, as Mr. Mendelsohn makes so vividly and poignantly clear. For Odets, the "mere" success of Eastern and academic literary acclaim, the appreciation by intellectual critics alone, could not constitute the bulging fulfillment of the American possibility. Not the violinist but the prize-fighter commands the attention of television's millions. American success naturally had to include Hollywood, as it had done for William Faulkner,

Ernest Hemingway, and Arthur Miller, in various ways. Like George Bernard Shaw's hell in *Man and Superman*, Hollywood is able to delude one with the sense of the easiest delights of Arcadia, a level of hell which even Dante did not probe down far enough to describe. A man of the theater to his very roots, Odets was his own best audience, able to persuade himself readily into suspending his disbelief, dulling that incredibly sensitive ear, blurring his fine instinct, confusing even more a sensibility that had already been blunted and contorted by party-line political convolutions and moral agonizing.

Mr. Mendelsohn concentrates on the facts of the matter, the body of Odets's work, its topology, Odets's own extended commentary about himself and his texts. We are extraordinarily fortunate in having Mr. Mendelsohn provide us for the first time with Odets's musings in such full form. Odets's very rapid rise and subsequent career, which cannot be described in any simple way as a fall, are here presented to us as a record. If there is tragedy in the document, we ourselves provide the design and movement. We have here, then, a full portrait of the artist as an American, subject to all of the pressures exerted both by society at large and by those particular personal and professional areas in which he chooses to operate.

Where are we to look for the essential Odets? In the early brilliant combination of successes, when three theaters on Broadway were simultaneously showing his work and he was emerging as the new voice of the American theater in the company of no less a personage than that of O'Neill? Or are we to find the essential Odets in the later figure, more shaded, more mottled, more mysterious, the brilliance gilded to flashiness, of the Hollywood and television years? Or in the quiet, lyrical wisdom of the late play about Noah, another man who lived through a lifetime of coping with the problems of being chosen for great things and of surviving great trials. As with any artist, any answer sufficiently based on the evidence can be persuasive. Mr. Mendelsohn's book provides the evidence in abundance.

Morris Freedman
University of Maryland

Chapter 1

THE BACKGROUND

*I*N AN INTERVIEW which he kindly granted me not long before his death, Clifford Odets made a statement that has taken on an added irony:

> We live in a time where you say something in one decade, and a decade later you're old-fashioned. They talk about me as a playwright, or *the* playwright of the Thirties. I've set down some of my best plays outside of the Thirties, and I'll continue, I hope, to do more of my best plays in the Sixties! What are they going to call me in the Sixties, when I produce three or four or five plays which will obviously have quality? What are they going to still call me, a playwright of the Thirties?

Odets' rhetorical question has now been answered: despite such fine plays as *The Country Girl* and *The Flowering Peach*, Odets will be remembered as the firebrand who ignited the American theatre early in 1935 with *Waiting for Lefty* and *Awake and Sing*. Because of his first four plays, Odets became known as a vigorous critic of American society, a reputation that was not completely deserved. In all his later work, in whatever form, on whatever theme, Odets remained associated with the "stormbirds" speech of *Waiting for Lefty*. That play became the ghost he could not escape.

1

A writer with the talent and the inclination to capital-
ize on the anger of a large segment of the playgoing public
could not have chosen a better year than 1935 for his
debut. Depression had tightened its strangle-hold on the
nation; audiences were often bitter or confused. Odets, an
unknown young actor with the Group Theatre, suddenly
emerged as a writer capable of capturing the imagination
of his socially conscious audiences. The late winter and
early spring of 1935 saw the productions of *Waiting for
Lefty, Awake and Sing,* and *Till the Day I Die.* On the
basis of these three plays, only one of which was full-length,
audiences and many critics hailed Odets as the greatest new
playwright since O'Neill.

Although Odets immediately established a reputation
as an angry champion of the proletariat, there was little in
his background to suggest either anger or proletarianism.
Odets was the first child born into a middle-class Jewish
family in Philadelphia, July 18, 1906. His father was a
relatively prosperous printer. Odets emphasized to interviewer Thomas Sugrue in 1935 that his background and
early life were "average middle-class American." Although
he grew up in predominantly Jewish neighborhoods in the
Bronx, where the Odets family had moved when he was
two, his family did not resemble in the least the Bergers of
Awake and Sing. He left high school in the eleventh grade
and found small acting jobs on the radio until, at the age
of twenty, he found a place as a juvenile in a group known
as Mae Desmond's Stock Company.

Odets' early acting career included such varied off-
Broadway experience as Harry Kemp's Poets' Theatre and
a one-act play group called The Drawing-Room Players.
But an opportunity to work as understudy to Spencer Tracy
in a short-lived production, *Conflict,* brought him to Broadway in March, 1929. Later that year he was hired by the
Theatre Guild. For the Guild he toured in various plays,

and in 1930 had his first real Broadway part, the juvenile lead in *Midnight*, a melodrama by Claire and Paul Sifton. Thus at the time that Harold Clurman and other young Guild insurgents began holding meetings to formulate plans for a new kind of theatre, to plant the seeds that were to spring forth the following summer as the Group Theater, Odets was an anonymous young actor living on little but his aspirations. In the fall of 1930 there were hundreds like him living in New York. He was twenty-four years old and had never considered writing as a career.

As a matter of fact, before his association with the Group, Odets' life provided few clues that would indicate a literary career. With one notable exception, his early reading seems to have been desultory and somewhat meager. The exception is Hugo, an author to whom Odets once paid homage:

> He is my literary and spiritual grandfather. I *love* Victor Hugo. Between the ages of, I guess, thirteen and eighteen or nineteen I must have read almost every novel that Victor Hugo wrote, but was particularly moved, beyond my awareness or comprehension, by his novel *Les Miserables*, which I read through perhaps twice or three times. As a matter of fact, this past July 18th was my 55th birthday, and I gave myself a present of a new edition . . . of *Les Miserables* and wrote in it "This will probably be the last copy I shall ever buy of this deeply beloved book." So Victor Hugo meant a great deal to me, still does, always will. Bombast and all. (Interview)

Charlie Castle, central character of Odets' 1949 play *The Big Knife,* is obviously a personal spokesman for Odets when he recalls,

> My uncle's books—for that neighborhood—I'll bet he had a thousand! He had a nose for the rebels—London, Upton Sinclair — all the way back to Ibsen and Hugo. Hugo's the one who helped me nibble my way through billions of polly

seeds. Sounds grandiose, but Hugo said to me: "Be a good boy, Charlie. Love people, do good, help the lost and fallen, make the world happy, if you can!" (Act I)

As to his early knowledge of dramatic literature, Odets on one occasion denied any close acquaintance with the works of Chekhov before 1935 and at another time admitted to only a spotty knowledge of Ibsen's plays and Greek drama. As to Shakespeare, Odets made an extremely revealing comment in a letter to critic John Mason Brown in 1935. "In my usual dilatory way," he wrote, "I have just discovered Shakespeare. What a wonderful artist!!! How privileged I feel to be able to read him with a mature mind instead of a schoolboy's impatience." (*Seeing Things,* p. 110)

As he grew older Odets began reading more extensively both in dramatic and non-dramatic literature. He was never, however, what anyone would call a widely-read man. His school was the school of life; people he knew provided all the source material and stimulation he needed. He became fascinated by art and artists, by music, by the film-making process, by television, and he remained an enthusiastic student of human nature all his life. In a very real way he was among the best educated of American playwrights without ever having finished high school. He seemed to soak up experience from everything he touched.

Typical of this process of education is a comment Odets made on Eugene O'Neill. Odets recognized that his style was alien to O'Neill's, but suggested at the same time that he had gained something intangible from the older man:

I admired O'Neill. I am influenced by O'Neill in terms of aspiration, in terms of becoming a big American playwright, in terms of being some kind of distinguished human being that people respect, in terms of shaking the audiences. He was part of the inspiration of what I call my Greenwich village days. At the time I got to Greenwich village, around

1925, most of the so-called great ones had gone. Floyd Dell had moved; George Cram Cook was dead. And O'Neill was part of this wonderful, glamorous world that a youth enters at the age of seventeen or eighteen. He was gone, but it was as if his fragrance, or the awesome sense of this man still lingered around the dirty alleys and streets. Macdougal Street meant the Provincetown Playhouse and Eugene O'Neill. In that sense I was influenced by Eugene O'Neill, but not directly by his work. (Interview)

One further secondary influence calls for special mention: music. Odets always loved good music, and, in fact, at one time thought he would become a musician. Harold Clurman mentions in *The Fervent Years* that one of Odets' early abortive attempts at writing was a play "about a genius of the Beethoven kind." Music certainly takes on significance in a great number of his produced plays: the grandfather's Caruso records in *Awake and Sing,* Steve's clarinet in *Night Music,* Pearl Gordon's piano in *Paradise Lost,* old Wilenski's concertina in *Clash By Night,* and the violins of Ernst Tausig in *Till the Day I Die* and Joe Bonaparte in *Golden Boy.* In his conversation Odets often turned to classical music for allusions and illustrations. More remarkable, it is clear from a number of his diary entries and notes now in the possession of Dr. Margaret Brenman Gibson, that Odets identified himself closely with Beethoven until his death in 1963.

But music and literature were of minor importance in Odets' career compared with the ferment and anxieties of the early depression years. As a troubled nation sank more and more deeply into an apparently hopeless economic depression, fads, gimmicks, and, occasionally, ideas were proposed from every side. The Thirties became the era of The Townsend Plan, Technocracy, Huey Long and Share-the-Wealth, Father Coughlin, Fritz Kuhn, and End Poverty in California (EPIC). An average of thirteen million Americans were out of work in 1932, and an American dream of endless prosperity had been shattered. Ten persons were killed and ninety wounded in the C.I.O.'s ill-fated attempt to organize the Republic Steel Company in Chicago. Nearly a quarter of a million persons took part in the great trek from the dust bowl states to California, leaving behind empty, dust-covered farms and homes. The bitter aftertaste of the economic upheaval led some persons to watch with unconcealed admiration as strong men rose to power in Europe and whipped their countries into action. Others began to look toward Russia and Marxist panaceas for guidance. Bombarded by prescriptions from both demagogues and sincere patriots of divergent ideologies, President Roosevelt, after his inauguration in 1933, sought to help the people of the United States achieve at least the minimum goals of better housing, more jobs, and social security.

Odets and the other "angry" writers — men like Dos Passos, Steinbeck, Farrell, Lawson—thrived in this crisis atmosphere. Taking their cue from Moscow-bred ideas on literature with significance, these authors became conspicuous in every field of writing during the Thirties. "The theatre is a weapon" became the battle cry of the militant left. With red flag waving, they rallied to the cause of workers' theatre so hopefully extolled by the ultra serious, self-righteous editors of *New Theatre*:

> The increasing importance of the dramatic arts as a stimulus to thought and action is evidenced by the remarkable growth of the revolutionary theatre, film, and dance during the past year. The strength and growing influence of the workers' theatre has alarmed the ruling class of every bourgeois country . . . for the slogan, "Art is a weapon of the class struggle," has penetrated the broadest strata of worker-artists the world over . . . . Despite the combined onslaught of that unholy trinity, Capital, State and Church, revolutionary theater workers the world over will continue the fight against war and fascism, for a social system in which

the arts and sciences serve not the Morgans and the Mellons, the Rockefellers and the Rothschilds, the Krupps and the Comite des Forges, but the mass of mankind. (September 1934)

The message is clear, doctrinaire—and idealistic. The writer (probably Herbert Kline) felt compelled to remind his readers monthly that the movement was making its presence felt. At the very same time, his typical articles always flayed the writers for not doing quite enough:

Unfortunately our art, our "weapon," has often been as blunt as our fight has been brave. Frequently we find ourselves lagging behind the high demands of revolutionary art. While worker audiences will tolerate amateurish work for a while, they will not tolerate work of a low level indefinitely. We must analyze the weaknesses of our work now, and begin an intense and immediate drive to remedy them, to raise our art to a new high level.

This double-edged approach finally wearied many talented playwrights and drove them to turn their backs on the left-wing slant.

While most American playwrights never fully succumbed to leftist ideology, many others gave themselves over to writing what they hoped was meaningful proletarian literature on a full-time basis. More noticeably than in any other field of American life, leftist ideas permeated the arts during the decade (though Himelstein is correct in pointing out that the radical influence is often exaggerated). Harold Clurman tells of further incidents which reveal this tendency toward proletarianism and anger. Concerning a talk he made one evening in 1931, he comments in *The Fervent Years* "It was my bad temper that was most appreciated and applauded. I did not realize then that we were entering into a period of controversy. It was my first lesson in the temper of the thirties." (p. 61) Again, concerning a Group Theatre production late the same year, this is his recollection:

> The last night of the play the balcony was packed. Each night the audience had grown more vociferous. But that night there was something of a demonstration in the theatre, like the response of a mass meeting to a particularly eloquent speaker. As the actors—surprised and moved— were taking the curtain calls, a man in the balcony shouted: "Long live the Soviet Union!" Franchot Tone, on the stage, shouted back, "Hurrah for America!" Both outcries might be described as irrelevant, but evidently there was something in the air beyond theatrical appreciation. (pp. 66-67)

Events like these, far off or eccentric as they may now appear in our era of more staid theatre manners, were almost commonplace in some parts of the New York theatre world then.

Nurtured in this highly-charged emotional atmosphere, Odets encountered the greatest influence of his crucial years, 1930-1935, in the Group Theatre, an organization whose ten-year story has been admirably recorded in *The Fervent Years* by Harold Clurman and in *Drama Was a Weapon* by Morgan Y. Himelstein. After some tentative experiments under the protective wing of the Theatre Guild, Clurman associated himself with Lee Strasberg and Cheryl Crawford to form the new theatre; in June, 1931, these three took a coterie of some thirty actors, including Odets, to Brookfield Center, Connecticut, where they studied and rehearsed all summer. That fall, September 23, the company presented its first production, Paul Green's *The House of Connelly*, at the Martin Beck Theatre. The critics were delighted and the Group was launched. Sharing in the organization's triumph with a very small role in Green's play was Clifford Odets (with his name, incidentally, misspelled *Odetts* in the Burns Mantle *Best Plays* listing of the cast). During that first season Odets also had parts in the two other Group productions, Claire and Paul Sifton's *1931* and Maxwell Anderson's *Night Over Taos*. In the next three seasons Odets had parts in four additional Group plays, including one of its rare commercial successes, Sidney Kingsley's *Men in White*. Odets ended his acting career as Dr. Benjamin in his own *Waiting for Lefty* in March, 1935.

His thorough grounding in the theatre unquestionably played a vital role in Odets' dramas. Odets was not given to flights of false modesty; therefore, it was a natural and honest reflection for him when he observed to Thomas Sugrue as far back as 1936, "I don't think I would ever have written a play if it hadn't been for the Group. And if I had it wouldn't have been so good. They helped me to assert my values." A quarter of a century later Odets had not changed his mind:

> My chief influence as a playwright was the Group Theatre acting company, and being a member of that company . . . . And you can see the Group Theatre acting technique crept right into the plays. I have often been accused of aping Chekhov, which is in no sense a *mean* thing. But the real truth is that with the Group Theatre I wrote not one or two leading parts with a lot of supporting players, but the early plays were written with equal size parts for equal size actors. . . . And that form was dictated by the composition of the Group. (Interview)

Odets might have added that this form was the direct result of Harold Clurman's vision. The Group Theatre was organized and guided throughout its stormy career by Clurman, Miss Crawford, and Strasberg. As set forth in *The Fervent Years*, the Group's general aims may be summarized as follows:

1. Actors should be trained and allowed to grow; the Group was to be a school as well as a production organization.

2. The actor and the playwright should be brought closer together.

3. A philosophy of life should guide the work of the Group and even pervade all the plays.

4. The *production* counts most; therefore, there should be no "stars."

5. A unified method should be employed by the triumvirate of directors in order to mold the actors into a single organism.

Financially, the directors were most interested in achieving the goal of a permanent acting company with a treasury to produce its own plays in its own ways; they wanted to pay the actors a standard salary throughout the season, replacing the normal feast-or-famine procedure employed by Broadway producers, by which actors are paid by the week only during a play's rehearsals and run. Today's Lincoln Center Repertory theater founded by Group member Elia Kazan and others, is but one offshoot of the Group theatre idea.

Artistically molded by Strasberg, the Group presented ensemble work which was overwhelmingly applauded, even when a particular play was not praised, by critics accustomed to the star system. Strasberg's techniques as a director and teacher were liberally borrowed, with minor modifications, from Stanislavsky. In the meantime Clurman apparently confined most of his early contributions to observing Strasberg and expounding much of the original *mystique* of the Group. The actors, Odets among them, thrived on the heady diet, feeling that at last they were able to mature as artists. They were no longer a "commodity" hired for one part and then out on the street making the rounds of casting offices again. As Clurman aptly put it, "Here was something new to most of the actors, something basic, something almost holy. It was

revelation in the theatre; and Strasberg was its prophet."
(*The Fervent Years,* p. 41) The fact that the Group failed
to achieve all its aims is immaterial. The influence of the
organization's personnel on today's American theatre has
far outdistanced anything ever envisioned by Clurman in
his most idealistic moments.

One sideline of the Group brought the organization an
unwanted type of publicity. Because the Group's leaders
were theoreticians and intellectuals even more than they
were pragmatic theatre people, they were naturally interested in the renowned Moscow Art Theatre and the
techniques of Stanislavsky. Clurman, Strasberg, Stella Adler, and other Group leaders likewise visited Copeau,
Meyerhold, and other distinguished European theatre
artists. This interest which on occasion led Clurman to
make pilgrimages to Moscow in order to speak to Stanislavsky, helped foster the distorted notion that the Group
theatre was little more than a communist cell. While
such comments were obviously unfair, it is equally obvious
that some members of the Group, including Odets, were
interested in Marxism to one degree or another. Clurman,
while emphasizing vigorously that the Group was in no
sense a communist-influenced organization, relates some
amusing anecdotes which shed light on the feelings of
many members. He notes that at one performance Morris
Carnovsky was guilty of a late entrance:

> When I inquired into the cause of this late entrance, some-
> thing almost without precedent in Carnovsky's career, some-
> one misinformed me, with a touch of malice, that he had
> been reading the *Communist Manifesto* . . . in his dressing-
> room and had thus forgotten his entrance cue. (*The Fer-
> vent Years,* p. 99)

On another occasion, J. Edward Bromberg wanted to quit
the company:

Bromberg pointed out, quite properly, that there was not enough for him to do around the Group then. He drew himself up to his full height (unfortunately insufficient for the occasion) and announced in an almost defiant voice: "Besides, I like workers," a statement that struck everyone as a bewildering non sequitur. (*The Fervent Years*, pp. 99-100)

Caught up in his own "I like workers" syndrome, Odets began his brief association with the Communist Party in 1934. Testifying before a Congressional committee in 1952, Odets disclosed his motivation for joining:

I believe at that time there were perhaps 15 or 16 million unemployed people in the United States, and I myself was living on 10 cents a day. Therefore, I was interested in any idea which might suggest how as an actor I could function as a working actor who could make a living at a craft he had chosen for his life's work. These were the early days of the New Deal, and I don't think that one has to describe them. They were horrendous days that none of us would like to go through again.

On this basis there was a great deal of talk about amelioration of conditions, about how should one live, by what values should one work for [*sic*], and in line with this there was a great deal of talk about Marxist values. One read literature; there were a lot of penny and 2-cent and 5-cent pamphlets. I read them along with a lot of other people, and finally joined the Communist Party, in the belief, in the honest and real belief, that this was some way out of the dilemma in which we found ourselves.

In the summer of 1935 Odets' political activity reached its sudden climax with a denouement that suggested comic opera more than Comintern. As leader of a group of writers and union officials he set sail for Cuba, ostensibly to investigate the plight of labor and students under the Mendieta dictatorship. The entire group was un-ceremoniously arrested upon arrival in Havana harbor, detained overnight, and sent back to New York on the first ship available the next day. The episode created a minor furor and probably, in the light of Odets' 1952 testimony, accomplished exactly what was intended: simply to direct attention to police state activities just off the coast of Florida. Details of the mission are recounted in the New York *Times*, July 3-July 7, 1935. Odets also co-authored with Carleton Beals, a pamphlet on the subject titled "Rifle Rule in Cuba."

That summer also marked the end of Odets' association with the Communist Party. Feeling that his creativity was being inhibited by attempts to pressure him into writing only party-line plays, he resigned after eight months as a member. The way he explained his departure (to the House Committee on Un-American Activities in 1952) is revealing:

> Mr. Odets: They would have liked to have had me write what they would call . . . "progressive plays." They would like me to write plays on what themes they would think would be burning issues of the day. I am sure, for instance, the Communist Party thought that the war in Spain was a burning issue of the day. . . .
>
> Mr. Tavenner: And they attempted to direct you in that course of writing?
>
> Mr. Odets: In the sense, sir, of saying, "This man is wasting his time writing about ordinary, middle-class life when he could be writing a glorious play about the war in Spain." It was in that sense that they would try to influence one, chiefly in that sense.
>
> Mr. Tavenner: Well, did you follow the suggestion? . . .
>
> Mr. Odets: I am afraid I never did.
>
> Mr. Tavenner: Why?
>
> Mrs. Odets: I didn't believe it. I didn't respect any person or any party or any group of people who would say to a young creative writer "Go outside of your experience and write outside of your experience a play." I knew that as fumbling as my beginnings were, and they certainly were, that I could only write out of my own experience, out of my own incentive. I couldn't be given a theme and handle

it. It was not my business. It meant to me, if I may say it this way, a loss of integrity. And so I persisted in going along on my own line and saying and writing what did come out of my true center. And whenever this happened, I got this violent opposition in that press and I became further disgusted and estranged from them.

In such a turbulent atmosphere Odets worked and flourished. During his early Group Theatre seasons, Odets, like several other members of the company, began to make some attempts at playwriting. Two of these early efforts are described by Clurman, who read them carefully and explained their shortcomings to Odets. The first concerned "a house in Philadelphia he had lived in, full of confused and unhappy young people." The second was the play previously mentioned about the Beethoven-like genius. These two works gave Clurman little reason to believe that Odets was about to become the Group's leading playwright. "It showed no trace of talent," he wrote about the latter play. Odets, agreeing with Clurman's appraisal, admitted many years later, "They were very sad affairs."

But with his third attempt, Odets managed something quite unexpected and quite extraordinary. Early in 1933 he completed a draft of a three-act play about a family in the Bronx; he called it *I Got the Blues*. That summer the Group members performed a segment of it in one of their practice sessions. However, the play, still in a rather rough version, was quickly forgotten while the Group prepared to open its third season with Sidney Kingsley's *Men in White*.

A little more than a year later, the Group Theatre was preparing its fourth season, and Clifford Odets was on the eve of his first rapid successes. Odets was in Boston where the Group was trying out Melvin Levy's *Gold Eagle Guy*. Hearing of a contest for one-act plays sponsored by the New Theatre League of New York, he came to Clurman again with the idea of a play based on a recent taxi-drivers' strike in New York. Clurman liked both the plot idea and the rather experimental form which Odets suggested; with that encouragement, Odets—in a manner now firmly fixed in theatre legend—returned to his hotel room and wrote *Waiting for Lefty* in three days. By the time this play was given its exciting reception the following January, the Group faced with the unhappy prospect of closing its season rather quickly on the failure of *Gold Eagle Guy*, had finally decided to do *I Got the Blues*. The play had now been thoroughly revised and re-christened *Awake and Sing*. Rehearsals began on *Awake and Sing* about a week before the off-Broadway presentation of *Waiting for Lefty*, thus setting the stage for Odets' bomb-like explosion upon an unsuspecting New York.

When *Awake and Sing* received its warm reception in February, the Group hastened to bring *Waiting for Lefty* uptown. Needing another short play to complement it, Odets wrote *Till the Day I Die* and, beginning March 26, 1935, the two plays formed a successful combination.

The Group Theatre had discovered its voice—strident as it might have seemed at times. Now the young playwright, an unknown on New Year's Day of 1935, suddenly found himself central character in a Hollywood type of success story. He was sought out for speaking engagements and the cocktail circuit. *Time* and *New Yorker* discovered him to be an interesting subject. Hollywood studios made their first overtures. Overnight he was a celebrity, with all the advantages and disadvantages that word suggests.

Soon after Odets returned from his Cuban expedition that summer, he finished work on *Paradise Lost*, the fourth play of his presented in a single year. Following its opening, he accepted a Hollywood contract and made the first of several trips to the west coast. Odets' first film script reached the public in the fall of 1936, but despite a lucrative contract with Paramount, his interest still centered on Broadway. He prepared *The Silent Partner* for the new season in 1936, but for a number of reasons it was not produced. The Group presented *Golden Boy* in November, 1937 and *Rocket to the Moon* exactly a year later. Meanwhile, Odets had married the exotic actress, Luise Rainer, at the beginning of 1937, but the marriage was a brief one. In the midst of his crumbling domestic life, Odets returned to New York in time for the culmination of the early part of his career, the Random House publication of *Six Plays of Clifford Odets*, with a brief preface by the playwright. The day he wrote the preface was his thirty-third birthday.

Looking back on the meteoric rise a decade later, John Mason Brown noted, with a great deal of truth, "Mr. Odets' career can be said to have got off to a poor start if for no other reason than that it started off too well. It did not work up to a climax; it began with one." (*As they Appear*, p. 168) In a reflective moment Harold Clurman likewise looked back on the entire process sadly:

> Our white hopes darken with the years. Their annihilation is implicit in their glorification. Effusive praise is not necessarily harmful to playwrights or morally wrong of the press. But the basis on which praise is bestowed and reputations are made is false. To call an artist the greatest of the year or, before ten years are out, the greatest of the decade, is critically as meaningless as calling him the greatest on Forty-fifth Street. Such encomia can have significance only as publicity designed to stimulate the box office. (*Lies Like Truth*, p. 42)

By the end of the decade, financial problems and artistic differences were hastening the disintegration of the Group Theatre. One more Odets work, *Night Music*, was produced by the Group early in 1940. Breaking with Clurman, Odets then wrote *Clash By Night*, which Strasberg directed, and which was probably destined for failure even if it had not opened its run at a most inauspicious time, December, 1941. At the end of 1942 Odets did an unsuccessful adaptation of a new Soviet play, *The Russian People*, and then departed once more for Hollywood, which he made his home base until mid-1948. In California Odets married Bette Grayson in 1943; they were divorced near the end of 1951. According to an interview with Seymour Peck in the New York *Times*, Odets was kept out of the armed forces by an old arthritic ailment, and when he applied to perform some kind of war-service writing project, he was rejected again on the grounds that he had been "a premature anti-fascist" (a wonderful wartime government euphemism for communist sympathizer).

Thus the playwright spent the war years in relative obscurity. Although he was making money, these years were probably Odets' most fallow period. His most satisfying project was the filming of *None But the Lonely Heart*, which he adapted from Richard Llewellyn's novel and which he directed as well. Other films followed, but then in 1947 the Hollywood world suddenly came crashing down about the heads of Odets and hundreds of others; first the California State Legislature and later the United States House of Representatives began the investigations and charges that split the film industry apart.

Disgust with the probes and blacklists that seemed to characterize post-war Hollywood spurred Odets into new activity. Odets left for New York, where his first play in seven years, *The Big Knife*, was a bitter attack on Hollywood commercialism, allowing the playwright somewhat immoderately to air his fury. *The Big Knife* was perhaps a good play with which to return to Broadway; its subject matter and its ugly temper made for discussion and controversy. But most critics were harsh with the play, asserting that it underscored many of the poor qualities of Odets' writing while muting the better ones.

Apparently calmer with *The Big Knife* out of his system, Odets spent more than a year quietly working on his next play. By this time exceptionally anxious to make *The Country Girl* a commercial success on Broadway (his last one having been *Golden Boy* in 1937) he determined not to trust the new play to any stranger's hands; as a result, the production marked Odets' debut as a Broadway director. *The Country Girl* began its highly successful run in late 1950, restoring him temporarily to the good graces of the critics and public.

Odets appeared before the House Committee on Un-American Activities in mid-1952 for two days of testimony. It was his decision to testify which brought a final rift in the already strained Group Theatre friendships: Odets and Kazan on one side of this emotional issue, Morris Carnovsky, Luther Adler and several others on the other. The acrimony surrounding the House hearings lingered, causing both Odets and his former associates pain and unhappiness many years later. In *Actors Talk About Acting*, for example, Carnovsky, writing several years after this episode, states: "I must not forget that the Un-American Committee [*sic*] and certain people in the theatre who are 'highly respected people'—I put that in quotes, for I don't respect them—made it necessary for me to be blacklisted for several years. I must not forget these things. These are part of life and living." It is clear to anyone who understands the Group Theatre experience both whom Carnovsky has in mind and why he feels so strongly. This unpleasant interlude, during which Odets for the first time publicly admitted his Communist Party affiliation, was followed by another period of quiet for almost two years.

Work on *The Flowering Peach* occupied Odets during this time, and in 1954 he directed its production. When the play closed after a short run, Odets returned to Hollywood in the spring of 1955. He remained and worked there until his death, having finally made his peace with the film world. His last six months were spent working on scripts for a new television series, The Richard Boone Show. He died suddenly on August 14, 1963 following stomach surgery.

Odets was no ivory tower writer. He was too deeply committed to people and their problems to create art for art's sake. "I have never been able to finish a Henry James novel," said Odets once. He went on:

> This may be some defect in me, but I don't think so; I cannot think so. The cult of Henry James with a certain kind of stable values. I think it's the stable values that interest people. You know, the fixed world, a closed world, a world that's not changing. We live in a time where you say something in one decade, and a decade later you're old-fashioned. (Interview)

Such a statement itself tells much about the concepts of the playwright. The world revealed in the plays of Odets is a dynamic, fluid, lived-in world.

Chapter 2

THE EARLY PLAYS: WRITTEN IN ANGER

i. *Waiting for Lefty*

*C*LIFFORD ODETS WAS at the peak of his political involvement when he wrote *Waiting for Lefty*, his first produced
play. This play of labor union strife is so often pointed to
as the typical leftist drama of the Thirties that the comment is as trite as it is oversimplified. The drama is militant, propagandistic, and strident, but, unlike so many of
the angry plays of the period, it is also frequently human
and touching. Part of the importance of the work certainly lies in the acclaim it received; since subtlety is not
one of the play's strong points, the fact that audiences were
able to lose themselves in such a direct assault is in itself
a good indication of the mood in that turbulent depression
year, 1935. Harold Clurman referred to the play as "the
birth cry of the thirties" and it is quite natural that the
drama has assumed for him a large, almost mystic halo.
Those less emotionally involved with the play may find
that in retrospect it is hard to become so excited as this.
Great drama is indestructible; *Waiting for Lefty*, for all
its merits, too often seems as dead as last year's newspaper.

There are many fine qualities about *Waiting for Lefty*,
not the least of them being that the author approached his

work with imagination and technique that far surpass what might be expected from a first play. As a result, *Waiting for Lefty* displays an artistry generally absent from other labor plays of the period. In a series of vignettes, sharply telescoped in time, the drama takes up the story of several characters associated in different ways with the proposed taxi drivers' strike. As Odets envisioned the structure, it was related to that of a minstrel show, with various characters emerging from the darkened stage into the spotlight to tell their stories. Although seemingly episodic in structure, *Waiting for Lefty* has a basic unity imposed upon it, first by the theatrical framework of the strike meeting and second by the gradually developed thesis that everyone involved is a part of Lefty.

Since *Waiting for Lefty* is a short play dominated almost completely by theme, the incidents of the theatrical frame are few. The drivers meet to consider a strike vote; various drivers come forward to relate recent incidents in their own lives and various stooges of management try to keep them under control; finally, word is received that Lefty, the awaited leader, will never arrive because he has been assassinated; this climactic event prompts one of the men to take the initiative and call for a strike vote.

But there is a double framework involved in *Waiting for Lefty*, and Odets never lets his audience forget the significance of his dramatic point. Time and again as the play builds its intensity, he wrenches the audience away from a scene with a violent reminder that there is a strike to be considered, action to be taken. The interplay between personal lives and collective action is masterfully handled: Joe and Edna need food for their children; a strike will provide it. The "young hack" can't afford to marry at all; a strike will enable him to do so. Dr. Benjamin is fired by an anti-Semitic hospital board; the clenched fist offers the solution. Each character is a fragment of Lefty, and the wait that is taking place is actually a wait for the sub-merging of the individual in the group.

Each scene adds to the intensity that is necessary for the play's success. By the end the pace is unrelenting, and all that remains is the achievement of a new leader's birth in Lefty's death. A crucial part of the message of labor solidarity is that many spring up where one dies. And so Lefty, very much alive in spirit, arrives in the body and voice of Agate Keller. Odets is doctrinaire, not existential. As a result, unlike the wait for Godot, the wait for Lefty is not in vain.

To present these events, Odets employs what may seem at first a peculiar assortment of characters. He is obviously striving to universalize his situation; undeniably there *were* members of the disrupted middle class and even some professional men trying to earn a few dollars as cab drivers in 1934. Still, the play seems rather oddly unbalanced. Of the five flashback scenes, three concern non-proletarians: a laboratory scientist, an interne, and an actor. The in-congruity of the situation is heightened, as John Howard Lawson later observed, by Odets' insistence on having the strike group addressed at the end as "stormbirds of the working class." But Odets could hardly do otherwise. The writers of the Left had little acquaintance with true work-ers. Odets was dealing with people he knew. Middle-class himself, he was directing his polemics at an audience that was also largely middle-class. Industrial workers who at-tended his performances did not need the prodding of such a theme; it was the middle class and the intellectuals who needed the lesson. Like so many other American authors of the period, Odets found himself attracted to proletarianism as a state of mind. It was a theoretical or spiritual involvement whose advocates accepted the task of committing their own group to the cause of worker soli-darity.

It is revealing that the scene with the unemployed actor is omitted in the Random House published version, *Six Plays of Clifford Odets*. Odets later stated that the reason for the omission was his decision that the problem was not sufficiently universal, that it had special meaning only for actors. Since the scene is the most militant and radical one in the play, a more likely reason for its omission was the calming of the playwright's extremism by 1939.

Waiting for Lefty is notable as the only one of Odets' plays to employ the theatricalist devices of direct address to the audience and actors planted in the auditorium. Both are well adapted to this play. While these techniques appear at first to belong to the anti-illusory theatre of Brecht or Wilder, Odets uses them for a totally different purpose. The basic assumption of the anti-illusionist writer is that the audience, aware that it is in a theatre, may constantly be reminded that it is viewing a play; the basic assumption of the illusionist is that effective drama can best be achieved if the audience forgets it is in a theatre and believes it is viewing not a play, but life. Odets, far from suggesting to the viewer that this is a play, works doubly hard to create the illusion of a strike meeting in a union hall. Almost in the manner of Pirandello, Odets blends the theatre and life, the imitation and the actual, so that the audience is never quite certain which is which. These techniques as well as the bare stage and the entire simplicity of the production made it admirably suited for use by small theatre groups or even for union meetings, and much of the play's success resulted from its use by such groups all over the country.

The dialogue of *Waiting for Lefty* first revealed Odets' tremendous power. In the true and touching words of Edna, wife of one of the taxi drivers, the dramatist demonstrates his exceptional ability for expressing the abstract of the class struggle by means of the concrete of family life:

You got two blondie kids sleeping in the next room. They need food and clothes. I'm not mentioning anything else—But we're stalled like a flivver in the snow. For five years I laid awake at night listening to my heart pound. For God's sake, do something, Joe, get wise. . . . I'm turning into a sour old nag. (i)

And a little later she exclaims, with even more power,

I know this—your boss is making suckers outa you boys every minute. Yes, and suckers out of all the wives and the poor innocent kids who'll grow up with crooked spines and sick bones. Sure, I see it in the papers, how good orange juice is for kids. But damnit our kids get colds one on top of the other. They look like little ghosts. Betty never saw a grapefruit. I took her to the store last week and she pointed to a stack of grapefruits. "What's that!" she said. My God, Joe—the world is supposed to be for all of us. (i)

On the other hand, Odets also displays his early tendency to end with an overwrought curtain speech, a passage excessively charged with emotion:

Hear it, boys, hear it? Hell, listen to me! Coast to coast! HELLO AMERICA! HELLO. WE'RE STORMBIRDS OF THE WORKING-CLASS. WORKERS OF THE WORLD. . . . OUR BONES AND BLOOD! And when we die they'll know what we did to make a new world! Christ, cut us up to little pieces. We'll die for what is right! Put fruit trees where our ashes are!

Such a speech may be exactly what an audience wanted to hear from a militant playwright; yet somehow on the printed page the ring is hollow. Most people go to a national political convention to cheer the speakers, no matter what they say or fail to say. In the same way, most of the audiences for *Waiting for Lefty* had to arrive at the theatre with a preconceived set of opinions, and when they heard the old familiar tune, "Workers of the world, unite," they were entranced mainly by the vigor with which it was shouted. Thus in his first play Odets showed his audiences tantalizing glimpses of effective playwriting embedded in large doses of pre-packaged Marxist stimulation.

ii. *Till the Day I Die*

In the play written to serve as a curtain raiser for *Waiting for Lefty*, when the latter drama was brought to Broadway, Odets abandoned the New York setting and characters he knew so well. *Till the Day I Die* represents the playwright's only excursion outside the United States for a setting until his non-localized *The Flowering Peach* many years later. (One minor exception is Odets' unproduced play about a Cuban rebellion written in 1938, which Odets called "the only really poor play I ever wrote." And it is interesting that he blamed its shortcomings on the fact that he was not really familiar with the people and the area he was writing about, a statement equally applicable to his earlier play about Germany.) Of Odets' eleven produced plays, *Till the Day I Die* is the slightest. As one of the first anti-Nazi plays written in the United States, its importance is historical rather than dramatic.

In this play as in *Waiting for Lefty*, Odets uses a series of brief scenes. However, the method employed is a straight narrative-sequential one rather than the series of vignettes used in the labor play. In seven scenes Odets depicts the degradation and death of Ernst Tausig, a Communist Party underground worker in the Germany of the new Fuehrer. Like so many political plays, this one makes certain assertions that are only slightly related to fact: one, that there was widespread organized opposition to Hitler within Germany; the other, that the Communist Party in Germany was the focal point and guiding light in that opposition. Unfortunately for the playwright, the march of events in Europe proved both of these ideas false. The latter belief dissolved especially suddenly with the signing of the Berlin-Moscow pact in the summer of 1939.

Apart from such political considerations, *Till the Day I Die* fails to be very convincing in its picture of an anti-Nazi underground. The playwright's constant emphasis on physical torture serves more to numb the reader than to make him angry or sympathetic. The mood of this play, in contrast to the steady heightening of mood in *Waiting for Lefty*, rapidly presents a suicide, a murder, and a hand-smashing scene. After all of this violence, the second suicide, that of the central figure, is almost an anti-climax. More important, the doctrinaire message which precedes the pistol shot, strikingly similar to the equivalent scene at the end of *Waiting for Lefty*, is again too emotional for the occasion.

The other aspect of the play which is most obviously contrived is the scene depicting one of the Nazis as a homosexual. It is weak because it is so completely irrelevant, adding nothing to either the plot or the characterization. If Odets is interested in demonstrating that all Nazis are perverts and all Communists noble, he fails badly.

At the same time, the play has its merits. Again Odets manages to put the anti-Nazi underground abstraction into human terms. One of the workers exclaims, apropos of nothing that has gone before, "I used to be crazy on tulip bulbs. For years I spent my weekly salary on them" (i). Ernst, the play's hero, is a violinist; thus the destruction of his hands is doubly immoral. (The same concept recurs in *Golden Boy*.) And again Tilly, Ernst's common-law wife, recalls small details of her early life:

> I had a nice coat once. I had a mother. I had a father. I was a little girl with pigtails and her face scrubbed every morning. I was a good child. I believed in God. In summer I ate mulberries from our own tree. In late summer the ground was rotten where they fell. (vii)

These and other poignant, humanizing touches show the playwright to advantage, but the net effect of *Till the Day I Die* is hampered by Odets' failure to invest his characters and his situation with a sufficient degree of verisimilitude. For a play which is framed in terms of historical realism, such a failure is disastrous.

iii *Awake and Sing*

Early in 1935, with the exciting success of *Waiting for Lefty* assured, Odets dusted off *Awake and Sing,* actually completed in draft form two years earlier. Now audiences had an opportunity to see what Odets could do in three full acts. The results were remarkably pleasing. If Odets disappointed those who were expecting another diatribe, *Awake and Sing* must have been a happy surprise to those who suspected that he was incapable of anything more than direct propaganda.

The story centers in the struggle of the two youngest members of the Berger household to escape their environment. In spite of what often appear to be overwhelming odds, the girl, Hennie, leaves at the end; she uses the escape hatch thoughtfully provided by the playwright. But her brother, Ralph, will remain, presumably to fight for a better life for himself and his generation. Some of the plot material employed by Odets left him vulnerable to valid comparisons to soap opera. Nonetheless, even this reliance on fairly obvious plot devices (an inheritance, an illegitimate child, a timely suicide) fails to destroy what is essentially a warm and vibrant picture of the struggles of a Bronx family.

Each character is important in this well-knit play, but apparently old Jacob—ineffectual as he must often seem—is Odets' spokesman. No one in the play pays the slightest bit of attention to Jacob's prophecies, even though each of the characters is to some degree a part of the general depravity of which he speaks. Even Ralph doesn't understand his grandfather; yet, at the end, Ralph comes alive in the death of the old man, thus fulfilling one of Jacob's key prophecies: "For years, I watched you grow up. Wait! You'll graduate from my university" (I). Further under-scoring the character's importance, the statement of the playwright's theme is given to Jacob who demands of his grandson, "Go out and fight so life shouldn't be printed on dollar bills" (I).

Underlying *Awake and Sing*, as in so many twentieth century plays, is a noticeable attitude of economic deter-minism: the evil is in the system, not in the people. The Berger household contains neither hero nor villain. Moe Axelrod is the character who best demonstrates Odets' attitude on this matter. A bitter disabled veteran, Moe sees clearly the need for escape. His cynicism and his hard shell cover, in true sentimental tradition, a sensitive heart. He is the detached, calm observer of life, able to see the foibles of others, yet unable to keep his own emotions in check when touched. In another perspective, Moe is a traditional character between the old (Jacob) and the young (Ralph). The generation that is really warped, Odets indicates, is Bessie's and Myron's; chained to their own bourgeois attitudes and slogans, they are leading a hopelessly false life. (They can squander fifty cents on Irish sweepstakes because someone a block away once won; Myron, the father, says, and perhaps even believes, "Merit never goes unrewarded" I). Because this group is so hope-lessly set in its ways, Odets skips over the middle genera-tion and confers Jacob's mantle of hope on Ralph and Hennie. That inheritance of hope motivates Ralph's opti-mistic utterance at the final curtain. Oddly, the character who leads the way for this rebirth is the embittered but romantic realist, Moe.

Much of the unfavorable criticism of the play centered

in the concluding scene, in which Hennie decides to desert her baby and run off with Moe. Krutch, for example, insisted that it was an afterthought, crudely tacked on. There is no doubt that the ending combines Odets' instinct for dramatic effect with his bent for intellectual propagandizing. The combination of Hennie's departure and Ralph's emotional affirmation of faith in the future, provides a characteristic conclusion for an Odets play. Some years ago, asked whether or not he would alter the ending if he were re-writing the play, Odets stated in a letter to me:

> I think *Awake and Sing* should stand as it is. It is true that on the part of the children in the family a "manifesto" is stated (and that the manifesto perhaps does not have the psychological density of certain earlier despairs) at the end of the play; but much in the first two acts of the play points towards the burgeoning insights on the parts of the young folks. What critics seem to carp at is the cultural (or ethical) meanings of the insights arrived at.

More recently, the playwright again reaffirmed a belief in the honesty of the ending. But he added a qualification which suggests that Odets grew to recognize that there are more factors involved in such a decision than there were a quarter of a century ago: "I believed it then, and I believe it now. I think I believed it more *simply* then." (Interview)

The situation at the end of *Awake and Sing*, considered objectively, would not seem to offer much chance for Moe and Hennie to live happily ever after; Odets did not write fairy tales. Yet optimism is present in the very act of their escape. With Hennie beside him there is a hope that Moe will lose his shell of bitterness and make something of himself in the new society. Moe's conflict has been strictly internal. The one Moe says, "A guy in France has the right idea—dropped his wife in a bathtub fulla acid" (I), while his alter ego can say, "A certain place where it's moonlight and roses. We'll lay down, count stars. Hear the big ocean making noise" (III). Moe has had much in life to make him bitter, but he is still capable of compassion. He points the way for Ralph and thus for all the new generation.

Much of what is best about Odets is on display in *Awake and Sing*. Even relatively minor characters such as Uncle Morty and Sam Feinschreiber are clearly and lovingly etched. Yet the most important quality revealed by Odets in this early play is to be found in the language. The playwright's ability to hear and transcribe the cadences of immigrant Jewish speech is firmly established in *Awake and Sing*. "You gave the dog eat?" (I). "You wanted to make for yourself a certain kind of world" (II). "But you should act. Not like me. A man who had golden opportunities but drank instead a glass of tea" (II). Equally well he hears Morty, now a big man in the garment district, as he employs his heavy-handed sarcasm:

> MORTY: He had Caruso. Who's got more from life?
> BESSIE: Who's got more?
> MYRON: And Marx he had.
> MORTY: Marx! Some say Marx is the new God today. Maybe I'm wrong. Ha ha ha. . . . Personally I counted my ten million last night. . . . I'm sixteen cents short. So tomorrow I'll go to Union Square and yell no equality in the country! Ah, it's a new generation. (III)

Morty refers here to a new generation, one of many such references in the play. This emphasis on a continuing lack of communication between generations adds a contemporary slant to *Awake and Sing*. At the latest revival of this play (at the Charles Theatre in Boston in the fall of 1967) it was this dimension of the play that saved it from appearing dated, that helped make it relevant to a contemporary audience.

As in *Waiting for Lefty* Odets ably employs the poet's

technique of suggesting much with something small. In such economy there is an inherent effectiveness clearly recognized by every fine dramatist. For Odets the whole concept of frustration in a Bronx tenement is expressed with a meaningful concrete object. "What the hell kind of house is this it ain't got an orange!!" says Moe (I). Ralph is often the self-pitying yet touching mouthpiece for such statements: "It's crazy—all my life I want a pair of black and white shoes and can't get them. It's crazy!" (I). Again, he berates his mother because he has never had skates, and Bessie, her pride severely wounded, responds in kind: "He didn't have skates! But when he got sick, a twelve year old boy, who called a big specialist for the last $25 in the house? Skates!" (II). In such a discussion neither party is right or both parties are right. The overtones of simple desire for escape from drudgery are present in all these lines.

Another aspect of Odets' dramatic craftsmanship is evident in the manner in which he uses anticipation. Jacob's suicide, for instance, is thoroughly prepared though not, fortunately, with Ibsen's heavy handedness. First, he is allotted the task of walking the dog on the roof; later Moe looks at a newspaper and comments on all the financiers who are jumping to their deaths. Having thus planted the literal plausibility of the suicide, Odets provides the emotional motivation in the senseless act of plain meanness committed by Bessie when she smashes Jacob's beloved records. Hennie's pregnancy is similarly hinted at when she returns sick from a trip to the movies. The plan to marry her off to the unsuspecting Sam is foreshadowed at the outset in Sam's pathetic gift of chocolate peanuts, unfeelingly received by Hennie: "Loft's week-end special, two for thirty-nine" (I).

Awake and Sing appears in retrospect to contain much of the ebullience of O'Casey's *Juno and the Paycock,* and the Odets play suggests O'Casey's in other ways as well. There is, for example, the remarkably astute use of idiomatic language, qualities for which both playwrights have been justly admired. But beyond that is the mood, the "state of chassis" that exists in both worlds: O'Casey's Ireland and Odets' New York are equally out of joint.

Only the ending, in spite of the playwright's insistence on its merit, seems forced and unreal. Ralph's sudden transformation, his rebirth, his passionate utterance of the call to arms are even less credible than Hennie's decision to topple normal conventions. Hennie's walkout is acceptable, if only in John Gassner's terms of "the libido acting up in an intense girl"; Ralph's rapid maturity, triggered by nothing more compelling than watching his sister leave her husband and child, is not as convincing.

iv. *Paradise Lost*

While it showed overtones of O'Casey, *Awake and Sing* also provided for audiences the first indication that Odets was evolving an American-Chekhovian style. As in Chekhov, not much that is overt really happens; the conflicts are toned down, the crises muted. The most startling physical action of the play is Bessie's destruction of her father's phonograph records. But if Odets' attraction to Chekhov was hinted at in *Awake and Sing,* it appeared in even larger measure in *Paradise Lost,* the fourth Odets play presented in 1935. His knowledge of the Russian master manifests itself in the plotting, the characterization, the dialogue, the theme, and even in the mood, all of which reflect not a slavish imitativeness, but an astute adaptation of Chekhovian mannerisms to an American milieu.

Odets' immediate reaction to the comparisons drawn by several unappreciative reviewers was purely defensive. Following the opening of *Paradise Lost,* he asserted angrily that he had never read *The Cherry Orchard.* But the playwright had brought the trouble on himself by writing a preliminary publicity release on the play which called direct attention to Chekhov:

> By the time I came to write . . . *Awake and Sing* I understood clearly that my interest was not in the presentation of an individual's problems, but in those of a whole class. In other words, the task was to find a theatrical form with which to express the mass as hero. . . . Our confused middle class today—which dares little—is dangerously similar to Chekhov's people. Which is why the people in *Awake and Sing* and *Paradise Lost* (particularly the latter) have what is called a "Chekhovian quality." Which is why it is sinful to violate their lives and aspirations with plot lines. (New York *Times*, Dec. 15, 1935)

In spite of a number of such protestations by Odets and Clurman, however, *Paradise Lost* clearly demonstrates Odets' close kinship with Chekhov.

The mood of wistful melancholy which pervades the play until just before the end and the frequent use of very adroit humor suggest Odets' conscious cultivation of Chekhovian atmosphere. Though Odets breaks the pattern in the final acts of some plays, both playwrights normally avoid emphatic curtains. Shunning climax, the first two act endings in *Paradise Lost* suggest only increasing futility. There are, as well, other obvious points of comparison. Violence is avoided. Both dramatists make extensive use of allegory. Furthermore, the repetition of certain lines by Odets' characters is reminiscent of Gaev's "Cannon off the red." (Clara says, "Have a piece of fruit," and Ben repeats "four stars" as a term of approbation.) Most of all, the characters speak in a vacuum, listen without hearing, respond unresponsively. Like their counterparts in Chekhov's plays, they wander in and out rather aimlessly. There is even an example of mysterious off-stage sound, so deftly employed in *The Cherry Orchard*: at the final curtain, as

Leo crosses the stage, "a short fanfare is heard without." If lingering on such comparisons is academic, disregarding them completely is dishonest. To ignore Odets' relationship to Chekhov would be to ignore an important facet of Odets' technique.

In Leo Gordon's household are Leo and his wife, three grown children, and an old family friend, Gus Michaels. Each has his problems, but these individual problems, like the characters themselves, tend to blur and agglomerate. Furthermore, each character seems unaware that his own problem is but another manifestation of the general decay of society, middle-class sterility, or outmoded values tenaciously clung to. Gus Michaels dreams of a return to the old days, the beautiful summer nights "before the Big War. . . . Oh, it was so beautiful in those days!" (II). Like Chekhov's Firs, he lives in the past, in reminiscences of Schoemacher's Ice Cream Parlor. And he holds his Masonic pin in almost the same reverence that the others show for Ben Gordon's little track trophy. Leo's values center in his books and in Emersonian slogans. He wonders what mysterious force is affecting his neatly-ordered universe: ". . . what is happening here? Once we were all together and life was good" (II). Sam Katz is concerned about his childless marriage. Julie Gordon lives in his own special dream world of stock market analysis, his aimlessness underscored by Odets in a stage direction: "He starts out one exit, but changes his mind and goes the other way. It doesn't quite matter where he goes is the intention here" (II). But most alarming of all the parts of the middle-class picture is the breakdown in Clara Gordon's morality; rather than face bankruptcy and disgrace, she is willing to agree to the arson proposition suggested by Leo's partner.

Thus the characters in *Paradise Lost* are intended to merge into a composite picture of a futile middle class. But two characters who stand out from the rest distinctively are Kewpie and Pike. Both are onlookers and commentators on the Gordons' society. Kewpie, the arrogant and ruthless taxi driver, like Yasha in *The Cherry Orchard*, believes in direct action. He knows exactly what he wants and how to get it. Pike, the furnace man, addresses everyone as "Citizen" in the quaint manner of the French Revolution. The playwright's radical spokesman in *Paradise Lost*, he also becomes Leo's guide and mentor.

What actually happens in *Paradise Lost* is relatively simple and relatively unimportant except as it combines with and underscores the theme. The picture that finally emerges is one of an entire household—in fact a miniature society— struggling to overcome the erosion of that society. Profoundly disturbed by what he considered the inability of the middle class to turn from the fetishes that surrounded it, Odets here attempted to portray an entire class floundering aimlessly, heedless of the fact that it is trapped by forces beyond its control. *Paradise Lost* might almost be subtitled "the education of Leo Gordon," although what Leo learns is not exactly clear. In the course of three years, Leo observes one son dying of encephelitis, another son killed in a holdup, a daughter frustrated in love because of economic conditions, a business partner of twenty-two years become an embezzler, and even his wife tempted by dishonesty under the pressure of the depression. Leo's learning process is painful, and perhaps the rather unsatisfactory ending—another of Odets' early, overwrought curtain speeches—is a direct result of the playwright's unwillingness to be more specific about what Leo intends to do with his newly-gained insight. Odets' brave attempt to raise Leo to tragic stature in the final speech fails badly. The acquisition of wisdom through suffering brings a fitting end to the reign of Oedipus; it is not sufficiently plausible for Leo Gordon.

The subplots add to the picture Odets is sketching. In

one, Pearl Gordon, the daughter of the family, finds she cannot marry Felix because in the depression a musician cannot get a job. The situation is a direct extension of the episode of "The Young Hack and His Girl" in *Waiting for Lefty*. In a more interesting subplot, Leo's partner, (who constantly and bitterly complains about his wife's supposed inability to conceive a child—"a woman with a mix-up inside"—) proves to be impotent. And still more interesting is the story of the elder son. Ben has been fed on a diet of ego-inflating lies all his life. His career as a track star and the entire flimsy structure of the Dale Carnegie cult of self-love make Leo and Ben Gordon the direct ancestors of Willy and Biff Loman. Some of Ben's dialogue leaves no room to doubt that Arthur Miller was well acquainted with this play when he wrote *Death of a Salesman*:

> BEN: But I saw Alfred Bond yesterday—the big A.A.U. official—he says not to worry, a swell berth waiting for me in Wall Street. Will we make money! All the books you can read, Leo. A concert career for Pearlie . . . And Gus can have a better stamp collection than the King of England! Just be patient.
> LEO: Who said anything to you, Ben?
> BEN: I'll make good!
> GUS: You certainly got that magnetism, Ben.
> LIBBY: My Ben can be anything he wants. (I)

Most of the characters worship Ben, and a small trophy from one of his track successes is the tangible idol. Yet Pearl sees her brother clearly enough to refer to him as a person "who thinks he owns the world because he won some medals. The great genius who never earned a nickel in his whole life" (I). Eighteen months after his bravado speech and marriage in Act I, Ben is dead, victim of a policeman's bullets in an armed robbery, victim even more of a peculiarly warped version of life.

The ending of the play is perhaps the most preposterous thing that Odets ever wrote. Leo Gordon's final speech must be included here only to point out how much Odets was on occasion capable of misjudging what an audience might tolerate. Leo, about to be dispossessed from his house, his business ruined by an unscrupulous partner, his son slowly dying, his other son already dead, gazes into the future and sees the glory of the promised land:

> Clara, my darling, *listen to me*. Everywhere now men are rising from their sleep. Men, men are understanding the bitter black total of their lives. Their whispers are growing to shouts! They become an ocean of understanding! *No man fights alone*. Oh, if you could only see with me the greatness of men. I tremble like a bride to see the time when they'll use it. My darling, we must have only one regret— that life is so short! That we must die so soon. Yes, I want to see that new world. I want to kiss all those future men and women. What is this talk of bankrupts, failures, hatred . . . they won't know what that means. Oh, yes, I tell you the whole world is for men to possess. Heartbreak and terror are not the heritage of mankind! The world is beautiful. No fruit tree wears a lock and key. Men will sing at their work, men will love. Ohhh, darling, the world is in its morning . . . *and no man fights alone!* (Clara slowly comes down to her husband and kisses him. With real feeling. Every one in the room, Leo included, is deeply moved by this vision of the future. Leo says): Let us have air. . . . Open the windows.

It is hard to realize that these lines are from the same pen that produced the action-packed and intensely dramatic *Waiting for Lefty* only a year earlier. If it requires a large amount of suspension of disbelief for a reader to accept Ralph Berger's idealistic curtain speech in *Awake and Sing,* it requires an impossible amount to accept it from Leo Gordon.

Paradise Lost was one of the most controversial of Odets' efforts. The actors enjoyed it, and Clurman, who

directed it, praised the play highly in his introduction to
the Random House edition. In his own 1939 preface, the
playwright admitted a preference for *Paradise Lost* over
his other early plays: *"Paradise Lost*, poorly received as a
practical theatre work, remains my favorite in this group."
But the audiences as well as the critics were unhappy with
the play. Odets tended to bleed easily when attacked and
to boil quickly when aroused. Of course, Odets was not
the only playwright to engage in an occasional feud with
the drama critics, but his was especially energetic. Odets
fought back by hitting at his detractors in a newspaper
article quoted by Clurman in *The Fervent Years*:

> The young writer comes out of obscurity with a play or two.
> Suppose he won't accept the generous movie offers. Why,
> that means he's holding out for more. Suppose he accepts—
> an ingrate, rat, renegade. . . . If he's written two plays about
> the same kind of people, everyone knows that that's all he
> can write about. But when he writes about a different class,
> he is told to go back where he came from and stick to his
> cast (or caste) . . . . Suppose he rapidly follows one play
> with another, why he's writing "quickies"! But if they come
> further apart, it is a sure sign he's already written out. If
> the reviewers praise him on Tuesday, it's only because they're
> gentle, quixotic fellows. But watch them tear him apart on
> Wednesday! . . . The young writer is now ready for a world
> cruise! (pp. 157-158)

But this strained sarcasm made little impression on the
group attacked; the New York critics are a notoriously
thick-skinned lot. Both Odets and Clurman probably expressed in their statements the normal protectiveness of a
parent for a homely offspring.

v. *The Silent Partner*

Odets' next play was never produced, a fact which always bothered the playwright. In his 1939 preface to the

Six Plays, Odets mentioned *The Silent Partner* fondly, stating: "Rightfully that play belongs in this collection in the place of *Rocket to the Moon*, for of the two it was conceived and written first. Revisions have changed it, but in terms of inner and outer progression, it belongs among the first six, part and parcel of a 'first-period' group." In an interview with John McCarten of *The New Yorker* he once referred to it as "the best labor play ever produced in this country or in any other country," and later he reaffirmed this opinion (adding the even more specific comment that it surpassed Hauptman's *The Weavers*).

The one scene published from *The Silent Partner* indicates that it is a more violent version of *Waiting for Lefty*. When one of the characters suggests an end to the strike, she is attacked by another of the wives:

> You might take a lesson from the lowly banana, Mrs. Finch— stick to your bunch or you'll get skinned! All of you listen . . . you've none of you died yet. A little hardship? Yes! But you've had that before. You been raised up to it and it comes easy and natural by now. Well grit your teeth and hang on a little longer. Stop naggin' your husbands. They're voting on the question right this minute up at the Labor Temple and they want you to be right with them and see this fight to a finish, no matter what they decide. Those of us really interested in our children will be with the men in that fateful hour when the showdown comes with the Company. First they said to us, "Accept or perish" and now they say, "Accept or be shot," Well, we won't bend the knee.
> — (*New Theatre and Film*, March 1937).

The dialogue of this single scene reveals that the play is a continuation of Odets' angry phase, a carry-over from *Waiting for Lefty* and *Till the Day I Die*. *The Silent Partner* was considered, discussed, revised, and re-revised several times between late 1936 and mid-1939, but it remained unproduced in spite of the playwright's confidence in it. Clurman has suggested why:

No play of Odets had a wider scope, a greater variety of characters, or more exciting scenes. But the play, intuitively
sound in its basic perception, was very weak in all its central
characters and situations. The maturity that the Italian
baker was supposed to possess was exactly the quality that
Odets himself lacked. His play revealed more instinct than
accomplishment, more rough substance than created form. I
spoke to Odets at great length about this. If he could imbue
these central characters with the life he meant them to have,
this would be his most important play and he would indeed
be the writer everybody hoped he would become. He needed
to work hard rather than to push the play into production.
Odets listened to me as if bemused. He was having his
problems with Luise Rainer. He was somehow unsure of
everything, more bewildered in a way than he had ever been
as the obscure young actor of our crazy company. Odets was
now his own greatest problem. (*The Fervent Years,* p. 174)

If arbitrary divisions are helpful, *The Silent Partner*
may be placed at the end of Odets' earliest writing period.
These years, from 1931, when he made his first efforts, to
1936, when he wrote *The Silent Partner* and completed
his first film script, saw Odets emerging as a dynamic
young writer with recognized ability. He was developing
a characteristic style and a personal set of artistic standards.
But he was still known and admired more for his anger
than for his ability. A small item in the New York *Times*
July 24, 1935 perhaps best illustrates the kind of reputation that surrounded him. With John Howard Lawson
and three other writers, Odets called on Luigi Pirandello,
who was visiting New York in mid-1935. Pirandello apparently wanted to talk about literature, but his visitors
were more interested in politics. Pirandello claimed that
"politics and social questions 'are of the moment' but that
'an artistic moment lives forever.' He insisted that Mr.
Odets' plays were good plays 'not because they are social,
but because they are artistic.' " The *Times* reporter, ap-

parently somewhat overwhelmed by the whole exchange, added, "The conference broke up with some rancor."[1]

[1]Lawson later reflected on the episode: "Our visit to Pirandello was a wonderful comedy of errors. He thought we were young admirers coming to render homage. As he gradually realized that we were in his Hotel Room to ask him why he accepted Musso-lini, (and he himself had urged that the press be present to witness our homage), his fury was wonderful to behold. What struck me about Pirandello at the time was his lack of any respect for serious problems. After all, he could have had the courtesy, and the decency toward American writers, to answer us with dignity and to defend his own point of view. But he was far too frightened, too eager to serve his masters, to handle the situation with even a mini-mum of self-control." John Howard Lawson to the author, April 30, 1962.

Chapter 3

THE MIDDLE PLAYS: IN MODERATION
i. *Golden Boy*

*I*N SHARP CONTRAST both to *Paradise Lost*, a commercial failure, and *The Silent Partner*, which was never staged, Odets' new play in 1937 brought money, new laurels, and a temporary return to the good graces of the theatre public. Perhaps because of the very success which attended it, *Golden Boy* was always held in some slight disdain by its author.

Golden Boy, one of Odets' best-known plays, is the story of Joe Bonaparte, who puts aside the violin and takes up boxing gloves. The Italian family of the play is similar to the Jewish family of *Awake and Sing*, and it is apparent that Odets feels back at home with Papa Bonaparte, Siggie, and Anna in particular. Detracting only slightly from these well-drawn characters are two others: Carp, an extraneous and rather tedious commentator who enjoys "slicing philosophical salami" with old Bonaparte, and Frank Bonaparte, Joe's older brother, the most out-of-place character in the play. Frank is a union organizer whose presence in the play may be only partially explained away by Odets' desire to show that fighting for justice is a socially acceptable goal, while fighting in a prize ring is not. It may be that Odets' penchant for denouncing "the system" was no longer interesting him sufficiently. Part of the problem also is a feeble attempt to enliven Frank's part with some unsuccessful humor that harks back to Sheridan's Lucius O'Trigger: "It's my little brother Joie, or I don't know a scab from a picket!" (I, ii). Whatever the reason, Frank is by far the weakest character in *Golden Boy*.

All of the play's action centers on Joe and the conflict within him. In thus directing attention toward his central character, Odets considerably narrows his earlier focus. No longer is he concerned with a mass struggle for escape from stifling conditions, no longer is there a middle class up against incomprehensible forces, and no longer is there a labor union group loudly clamoring for arms. While it is undeniable that Joe's desire for money and all it can buy results from what the playwright obviously considers an American malady, the disease is shown in the context of a brash young fighter rather than an idealized class consciousness. In true melodramatic fashion, the sides are clearly drawn up in terms of right and wrong, with Joe's career as the reference point. Mr. Bonaparte, Tokio, and Lorna are interested in Joe himself; Eddie Fuseli, Moody, Roxy, and even Siggie are interested only in what they can get from Joe.

Golden Boy demonstrates Odets' maturing sureness of technique. Joe's violent end is carefully prepared for several times during the early part of the play. Tom Moody, talking about some of his early finds, recalls, "Those were the days when I had Marty Welch, the heavyweight contender—Cy Webster who got himself killed in a big, red Stutz" (I, i). Later, Joe declares, "Those cars are poison in my blood. When you sit in a car and speed you're looking down at the world. Speed, speed, everything is speed—nobody gets me!" (I, iv). Still later the reader learns that Joe has bought a Deusenberg (II, i), and so his fate is clear. Other devices employed in *Golden Boy* show Odets' intimate knowledge of the theatre. Background noise is used effectively in the two dressing room scenes. The clanging bell and the roar of the crowd, hungry for action, provide an exciting chorus for the on-stage events. Odets also has his musician-pugilist play his violin off-stage; likewise, all the actual sparring and fighting takes place off stage in order not to tax the ability of the actor or the credulity of the audience. But the playwright shrewdly allows Joe one sudden use of his fists in plain view of the audience (II, iv).

One other aspect of any playwright's technique should be considered at this point. Dramatic irony never receives major stress in an Odets play, yet it is employed deftly in *Golden Boy* as well as in several other plays. There is the wait for Lefty, with its predictable outcome. In *Till the Day I Die* Carl Tausig is destroyed by a rather inflexible code that he has helped to create. Julie Gordon in *Paradise Lost* is manipulating stocks on paper in fantastic get-rich-quick dreams while he is dying of encephelitis. Bernie Dodd in *The Country Girl* sets out to rescue Frank Elgin from alcoholic degradation and does such a thorough job that in the process he loses a more important objective, Frank's wife. All of these examples are incidental but important in the texture of the plays. In *Golden Boy* (III, ii) Joe wins his biggest fight and then learns that he has killed a man to do so; again, at the end of the play, the vultures are busily arguing over the division of the spoils when they learn (as the reader must certainly realize already) that Joe is lying dead on some highway. But the best use of dramatic irony in the play—in fact the strongest use that Odets ever made of it—occurs at the end of Act II. The scene culminates with the news that Joe has quit trying to protect his hands, has won his fight with Lombardo decisively, has in fact become the "tiger" desired by Eddie Fuseli. But in doing so, he breaks his hand, thus symbolically renouncing his father and any last hold that creative artistry has on him. With a heavy pencil Odets underscores the horror of the situation. While his sickened father watches, Joe displays only a masochistic pride in maiming his fingers, bringing a strong climax to a well-knit scene. The irony is stressed in the concluding stage direction: "Joe has become a fighter. . . . Joe begins to laugh loudly, victoriously, exultantly—with a deep thrill of satisfaction." Joe has indeed achieved his victory, but at a terrible cost. Nevertheless, perhaps because the dramatists of the Thirties tended to see life in terms of environmental influences rather than in terms of Fate, dramatic irony is never a dominant consideration in an Odets play.

In some plays Odets' dialogue, which combines the argot of the gangster with frequent bursts of impassioned lyricism, sounds out of place and false. Such a combination seems more appropriate to *Golden Boy* than to any of his other plays (except perhaps *Night Music*) because the nature of Joe's conflict necessarily places him in the world of both creative sensitivity and ruthless destructiveness. Joe Bonaparte, like Moe Axelrod of *Awake and Sing* and Kewpie of *Paradise Lost*, can be callous or warm, tough or lyrical, depending upon the situation. Describing what music means to him, he can say:

> With music I'm never alone when I'm alone—Playing music . . . that's like saying, "I am man. I belong here. How do you do, World—good evening! When I play music nothing is closed to me. I'm not afraid of people and what they say. There's no war in music. It's not like the streets. (I, iv)

A year later he is not only dressing like the gangster, Fuseli, but is also talking like him: "I wouldn't look at you twice if they hung you naked from a Christmas tree!" he tells Lorna (II, i). But the realization that he has killed a man wrenches Joe back to a sudden understanding of himself.

That understanding fuses the lyric with the tough side of his nature in his final exit with Lorna. The speeches of affirmation, so much like Ralph's at the end of *Awake and Sing*, are unmistakably Odets' in their exuberant rhetoric:

> LORNA: We have each other! Somewhere there must be happy boys and girls who can teach us the way of life! We'll find some city where poverty's no shame— where music is no crime!—where a man is glad to be himself, to live and make his woman herself!
>
> JOE: No more fighting, but where do we go?
>
> LORNA: Tonight? Joe, we ride in your car. We speed through the night, across the park, over the Triboro Bridge—
>
> JOE: (taking Lorna's arms in his trembling hands) : Ride! That's it, we ride—clear my head. We'll drive through the night. When you mow down the night with head-lights, nobody gets you! You're on top of the world then —nobody laughs! That's it—speed! We're off the earth— unconnected! We don't have to think!! That's what speed's for, an easy way to live! Lorna darling, we'll burn up the night! (III, ii)

It is hard to dispute John Mason Brown's assertion about *Golden Boy*: "More often than is comfortable Mr. Odets' new play invades the provinces of the pulp maga-zines." (*Two on the Aisle*, p.220) But in spite of such criticism and in the face of its author's moderate disdain, *Golden Boy* is too well written to be dismissed lightly. Significant or not, this play shows Odets at his peak in sureness of technique and mastery of his craft.

ii *Rocket to the Moon*

Odets followed the successful *Golden Boy* with *Rocket to the Moon*, a drama which shares with *Paradise Lost* a middle-class hero who achieves a sudden new maturity and insight during the course of the play. Ben Stark is a dentist with middle age creeping up on him. He is beginning to

realize, after ten years, that his marriage is less than satis-
factory. Thrown into daily proximity with a pretty secretary who is looking for love to fill the void in her life,
Stark predictably decides that the time has come for a last
fling. But Cleo Singer, the secretary, has another ardent
suitor, Ben's father-in-law. In the end, Cleo is faced with
a choice not unlike Hennie's in *Awake and Sing*, Lorna's
in *Golden Boy*, or for that matter Shaw's Candida. Cleo's
decision, which marks the climax of the play, differs from
that made by any of her predecessors; she rejects both men
and goes off on her own.

This triangle sounds, in such a summary, rather ordinary, and indeed the weaknesses far outnumber the
strengths in *Rocket to the Moon*. The play is enlivened,
however, by the presence of one of Odets' finest characters,
the father-in-law. An elderly widower with unhappy re-
membrances of his marriage, Mr. Prince constantly displays a suavity which he combines with conscious play-
acting. He is cleverly rakish in his pursuit of Cleo, his
failure to win her resulting only from her persistent ro-
manticizing of the whole situation. (There was divided
opinion within the Group on this ending; Clurman even
notes that Luise Rainer, Mrs. Odets, thought "that the
little girl ought to accept the offer of marriage proposed by
the play's old man." *The Fervent Years*, p. 219.)

The other characters are less interesting, suffering perhaps in comparison to the urbane Mr. Prince. His daughter, Belle Stark, despite the author's attempt to inject sympathy into her part, remains cold and unappealing. She
hates her father, supposedly for his disloyalty to his dead
wife, but her keen distaste for Prince, the warmest character in the play, does nothing to aid the reader's opinion of
her. More important, she is depicted as a restraining influence on her husband's ambitions; when he wants to accept an offer to move to a different location—admittedly a

gamble—she is the one who vetoes the proposition. Belle's psychological makeup is complicated by the frequent references to the fact that her only pregnancy ended with the child stillborn; yet any compassion which her loss might awaken in the reader is quickly dispelled by Belle's morbid insistence on remembering this event as an "anniversary": "Three years ago this morning. I had him, I felt I had him" (I). Her psychological problems unquestionably stem from this traumatic event as well as from the unfortunate marital relationship of her parents, but it is the shrewish side of her nature rather than the sympathetic side which is more often on display.

Stark himself is not much more than an easy-going, almost milquetoast sort. He is intentionally kept undistinguished by the playwright, but the very fact that he is usually so colorless makes his occasional outbursts of passion that much less credible. Somehow Stark is made wiser or ennobled by his brief summer of fierce attachment to Cleo:

> For years I sat here, taking things for granted, my wife, everything. Then just for an hour my life was in a spotlight. . . . I saw myself clearly, realized who and what I was. Isn't that a beginning? Isn't it? (III)

But he ends the play with his favorite phrase, "Sonofagun! What I don't know would fill a book!" Granting that this final word is considerably more probable than the last speech of *Paradise Lost* (in which, in Odets' most strained metaphor, Leo Gordon envisions a Utopia where "No fruit tree wears a lock and key"), a reader might still be inclined to ask, "So then what?" Dr. Stark may be an admirably exact portrait of a middle-class dentist, but he is so unheroic that he becomes nearly uninteresting as well.

Cleo's is a considerably more complex case. Odets' sudden shift of emphasis away from Stark and to Cleo is responsible for making the play's structure appear faulty. Cleo is presented as a shallow and stupid young woman and —even worse—as a poseur throughout most of the play. For this reason it is difficult to accept a number of things that happen. Stark perhaps has reasons for succumbing to her good looks. Prince has less reason. But the change in her character, her sudden emergence near the end as a girl with a clear head and a will of her own is a bit hard to explain. First impressions of Cleo are almost completely negative. She overdresses; she brags of a family background that is obviously only a product of her imagination; she steals Prince's witticisms in order to appear clever for Stark; without considering the consequences, she sets her sights on winning her employer's affection; she shows her ignorance in the most exaggerated ways that the playwright can devise: "Do you know something? I can't read Shakespeare—the type is too small" (II, i). Or again, "An important person once told me Mr. Rockerfeller—you know, that one, his father—he had a silver windpipe. With all that money! It goes to show you" (II, i).

Suddenly, half way through the second act, the playwright abandons the shallow character he has been building and starts to create a new Cleo, a sympathetic one, one who is, in fact, to become the central character of the last part of the play. The reader is compelled to shunt poor Ben and his trials into the background and to ask himself instead what is going to become of this unhappy young girl and her search for love. Odets begins the shift in focus through the use of psychoanalytical stage directions, in the manner of Shaw (but without Shaw's facility): "Alas, she is not yet wise in the ways of the world and the creatures therein." "Suddenly she flings her arms out, stretching on her toes. She is embracing the world!" "Note: Cleo, in her contact with those she thinks 'superior people,' is often afraid of repudiation on one score or another. This is so in her relationship with Stark. For this reason she seldom fully extends the power she feels over him. This gives most of her impulses and gestures a contained tentative quality; an impulse is seldom fully released" (II, ii). Despite these attempts to build up Cleo's psychological density, the close reader of the early part of the play is not going to be very favorably inclined toward this character.[2]

Cleo is a favorite type for Odets, one of the many lost youths who people his plays. But none of the others employs such an unsympathetic pose. Insecure, lonely, lost in the New York morass, Cleo constantly reminds any listener that she is searching for love. "Don't let me be alone in the world, Ben," she cries (II), but it is never clear whose version of love she is seeking. Prince tells her bluntly that she is pursuing story-book love. Even at the end, when her vision is exalted by Odets in one of his patented idealistic speeches, it is hard to imagine Cleo looking beyond the level of a Hollywood Prince Charming who will ride up and carry her away on a white steed. "None of you can give me what I'm looking for: a whole full world, with all the trimmings!" Hollywood's formula is simple and sufficient; Cleo buys the entire package.

The final impression of *Rocket to the Moon* was perhaps best summed up by George Jean Nathan, who leveled

---

[2]In the summer of 1962, when Odets saw an early draft of my comments on Cleo and Ben, he took time out to write a fine and characteristic rebuttal. While admitting that he now felt that Cleo was perhaps overdrawn, he defended her vigorously. Typically, he stressed the American optimistic idealism of his heroine. He considered both Cleo and Ben as typical Americans and chastised me for being too harsh on them. He even claimed to see in these characters the salvation of America. To his lasting credit, Odets was still in love with people.

a penetrating eye on the play and asserted that its thematic content might be stated as follows:

1. A very young girl can have little in common with a man old enough to be her father, however rich he may be.
2. Modern conditions are hostile to the perpetuation of true love.
3. Only by carefully nurturing love may love be made to flourish and endure.
4. Marriage must be an understanding partnership.
5. A marriage blessed by children is happier and more permanent than one not so blessed.
6. Emotional and sexual experience broadens one and makes one's life fuller.
7. What a young woman seeks is true love and in her search she is often frustrated.
8. Extremely hot weather is not especially conducive to sexual activity.
9. And so on. (*Encyclopaedia of the Theatre,* p. 289)

Such acidity did nothing to endear Nathan to Odets, and there is certainly reason to agree that this type of criticism is not helpful to a young playwright. Even year later the mere mention of Nathan was sufficient to arouse Odets to a burst of anger: "He was a first-class phoney." (Interview) At the same time, most readers will probably find themselves on Nathan's side in the case of *Rocket to the Moon.*

iii *Night Music*

Eight months after the production of *Rocket to the Moon,* the Random House edition of the *Six Plays* appeared. In his brief preface Odets attempted to draw a line after *Rocket to the Moon* and so end a "first-period" group of plays. After praising *Paradise Lost* and discussing *The Silent Partner* briefly, Odets proceeded in his own exuberant manner to place himself at the starting line in a new period of development:

When these plays were written it was almost impossible for me to do more or differently with them. Much of them was felt, conceived and written out of a personal need. Now after the fact, after the melancholy facts, the writer is a better craftsman, his horizon lifting wider. That temptation to improve upon these plays is often present. Nevertheless, none has been rewritten in part or whole: let them stand, crudities and all, as a small parade of a young talent discovering and shaping itself. If you have acquired by now the distressing sense that I am situating myself historically, correct! Talent should be respected.

This paragraph, so typical of Odets' egoistic style, shows the playwright bravely attempting a task that few authors will accept. Most are content to leave such analyses to the critics.

Odets' next play proved to be his last for the Group, and that organization was itself soon to be dissolved. *Night Music* is easily the most neglected of Odets' better plays. Unfortunately produced during the height of the Saroyan vogue, *Night Music* was pounced on by the New York critics as second-rate Saroyan rather than first-rate Odets. Several critics, puzzled by the fact that Odets' plays were looking less and less like *Waiting for Lefty*, made the comparison. Brooks Atkinson's statement in the *Times* was typical: "Now that Odets writes like Saroyan, Doomsday is near." Closer examination reveals, however, that the similarities are not basic to Odets' plays and, further, that there is nothing about the style of *Night Music* that had not been part of Odets' technique all along.

The innocent characters and the large number of "types" who populate Odets' Manhattan helped make the comparison to Saroyan natural. The odd characters in the park and in the lobby of the Hotel Algiers are somewhat similar to Saroyan's bar group in *The Time of Your Life*; yet Odets had used such minor characters in much the same way in *Paradise Lost* and *Rocket to the Moon*. Certainly the pure and simple central figures of *Night Music* are not new for Odets; Ralph Berger and Joe Bonaparte are among the younger innocents, Ben Stark and Leo Gordon among the older ones in earlier Odets plays. Critics tended to overlook an essential difference in tone between the two playwrights. Odets never relied on whimsey as a dominant mood in his plays, while Saroyan insisted upon it.

Some of the critical reaction to *Night Music* indicates why young playwrights grow old quickly. The reviewers for the New York dailies could find little to admire. Of this frankly simple play, one of them (George Ross in the *World Telegram*) wrote: "Its complexity is such that often you cannot be quite sure that *Night Music* is not the collaboration of Mr. Odets, Mr. Rice and William Saroyan, for it is in turn plaintive, whimsical, sunny, stark and brooding and at other moments, it is safe to be brash enough to say, it is just plain goofy." Atkinson, normally friendly to Odets, was very disappointed. John Mason Brown, then critic for the New York *Post*, was apparently unhappy about the calming of Odets' anger. And George Jean Nathan, always delighted at another opportunity to harass Odets, gleefully restated a favorite opinion:

> Clifford Odets, the hope that was white, at least in the view of more critics than you could shake a stick at, is decreasingly living up to his early anointers' sanguine expectations. His newest play, *Night Music*, must give them renewed and painful pause. . . . [*Night Music*] talks too much at the wrong time, and it suggests, as certain of his other plays have, a man volubly and indignantly waiting for an ideational street-car that never shows up. (*Newsweek*, March 4, 1940)

Loosely episodic in its structure, *Night Music* chronicles the meanderings of a brash young wanderer in New York. Steve Takis is without roots but in search of them. Constantly rebuffed in life, he has built up a strong defensive attitude to protect him from becoming involved with other people. So it is that when Fay enters his life, offering him the love he needs, he almost refuses to recognize its presence. But if Steve is another lost youth, he is a far more engaging one than Cleo Singer. Cleo's search for affectionate response seems tawdry, while Steve's never does. Both characters use make-believe to cover hurts in their early life, but Cleo's deceptions seem to be deliberately designed only to gain a hold on Dr. Stark. Whatever his faults, Steve wins the reader through the very boldness of his masks. His independent ways—often bordering on inexcusable rudeness—make him an oddly likeable character. A welcome foil for Steve is Fay Tucker, who possesses a softness and a sincerity lacking in any previous Odets ingenue. By comparison, Lorna Moon in *Golden Boy* appears badly tarnished, Hennie in *Awake and Sing* cynical, and Cleo self-seeking. Only Georgie Elgin in the much later *The Country Girl* approaches Fay in warmth among Odets' younger women.

The third principal character is one of Odets' happiest creations. Detective Abraham Lincoln Rosenberger is a combination of philosopher, guardian angel, and raissoneur. However, A. L. Rosenberger cannot be considered a whimsical sort of "good fairy" or genie in the bottle; he is a solidly conceived person with an understandable amount of impatience with Steve and a very real ache where the cancer is catching up with him. It is partially because of that cancer that the detective takes Steve's part when he learns that the boy's mother died of the disease. And it is partially because Rosenberger sides with Steve that the reader does also:

ROSEN-
  BERGER: These higher class diseases are international,
    like music.
LT.: Don't feel bad, Abe.

56

ROSEN-
  BERGER: I don't feel bad. (After a pause) And yet, with
    all his noise, he [Steve] makes a good impression.
    No? (I, i)

Taking an interest in the young couple, Rosenberger follows them around, hovering discreetly in the background,
offering advice when it is needed, sending sandwiches to
their rooms, and warding off the various evil spirits that
inhabit New York City. But his most important act is to
push them out of the nest and make them fly on their own
when they are ready. Having prepared them slowly for
the moment of their independence, Rosenberger wishes
the youngsters well in a beautiful valedictory:

  I'm tired, Takis. . . . Three days I watched you fighting
  shadows, so young, so strong in the heart. I'll tell you both
  a secret: no old man can rest if you don't use your health
  to fight, to conquer disease and poverty, dirt and ignorance.
  Go back to the city, boy and girl, sweet and sour. . . . You
  had the wisdom and foresight to be born in the twentieth
  century. Go, go with love and health—your wonderful
  country never needed you more. (III, ii)

Once again Odets signs off with a trademark. Yet this
speech—hard to believe when young Ralph utters it at
the end of *Awake and Sing*, impossible to believe from the
solid burgher, Leo Gordon, at the end of *Paradise Lost*—
somehow sounds entirely plausible coming from the almost
saintly detective.
  The speech pattern used by the central figure, Steve,
is a cleverly concocted blend of bravado and embarrass-
ment. No one in the play is much fooled by Steve's bluster,
and all seem to tolerate it, to allow him his mask, until the
tranquil Fay finally loses her patience with him (II, v).
Her anger breaks through his barrier, and the reader is
allowed to see the real Steve, a Steve he has suspected exis-

ted all along. But many clues are provided along the way concerning Steve's true nature. Not only the observations of the knowledgeable detective, but also the actions and speeches of Steve himself point up his real character. His almost exaggerated sense of chivalry causes him to blush frequently and apologize to Fay for his swearing. Time after time his feeling of inferiority gets the upper hand and he retreats in the face of Fay's attacks:

> STEVE: You're a menace to shipping . . . an idiot girl! When I'm hit that way it's like my mother died. . . . I'm off my top! Do you hear? You hear me tellin' you?!
> FAY: Steve, don't talk that way . . . !
> STEVE: Don't start with no spider, Miss Muffett—you'll be in a grave before you know it!
> FAY: Steve, excuse me—I'm sorry. . . .
> STEVE: An I a bum in the park to you? Am I?
> FAY: Don't look like that, Steve—excuse me.
> STEVE: (Shaking her) Answer me! Don't stand there like a saxaphone, waitin' to be tootled! . . . Why don't I tear you apart?! Why don't I kill you and the infant mortality goes up?! (Dropping her arms) Why don't I kill myself? What am I good for? Who needs me? Who wants me? . . . (Bitterly, his voice choking) Why don't I swim far out in the ocean and never come back? Why don't I do that quaint little thing . . . ? Who'd know? Who'd care? Suitcase Steve is dead! Who'd give a damn!
> (II, iv)

This typical exchange between the young people suggests the odd idiom of Odets' hero. His speech pattern is a natural evolution of the "tough guy" lyricism already noted in such characters as Moe Axelrod and Joe Bonaparte.

When *Night Music* was revived in 1951, Harold Clurman was drama critic for *New Republic*. As director of the original production, he was thus in a unique position to judge the play from his new perspective. That he still admired *Night Music* is obvious from his review. Unhappy with the failure of the audience to accept the play, Clurman wrote:

> There is no preachment—except on behalf of the most classic values and an almost old-fashioned, flag-waving American-ism. Yet the majority of our theatregoers . . . either do not recognize *Night Music* as a play or do not understand what it means. The reason for this is that Odets takes for granted that we all recognize our homelessness, that we all believe the rootlessness and disorientation of his hero to be typical. (April 30, 1951)

Whatever the reasons for its failure (twice) as a theatre piece, *Night Music* is a moving drama. Written with warmth and liveliness, this underrated work is a sincere expression of homelessness and confusion that ends on a buoyantly optimistic note. It stands as one of Odets' finest achievements.

iv. *Clash By Night*

If *Night Music* is Odets' most neglected full-length play, *Clash By Night* is probably his least consequential one. The play is marked by a return to the *Rocket to the Moon* triangle involving very ordinary people. Once again two lonely characters are thrown together in a situation which, like that of *Rocket to the Moon*, is predictably going to lead to a sudden love affair. And once again the hot wea-ther is considered by the playwright to be a catalytic agent for violent passions.

Odets presents as his central character in *Clash By Night* Mae Wilenski, who is chafing under the dull con-finement with her husband, a good-natured if somewhat stupid carpenter. Mae is interested in freedom and is not content to settle forever with Jerry into the hum-drum existence of lower middle-class life on Staten Island. She is stimulated by the introduction into the house of a boarder, Earl Pfeiffer. Earl, somewhat like Steve Takis, hides his loneliness and insecurity behind a mask of bluff; his facade is that of the "hail fellow well met." The mutual attraction grows rapidly, and Mae and Earl are drawn together in a way that leads predictably to violence.

The playwright establishes his mood very well. Lethargy induced by the heat is conveyed admirably in the first scene as the characters sit drinking beer on the front porch, their speech ordinary and aimless, their thoughts centered on grasping somehow at a breath of cool air:

> JERRY: Look at it! The moon comes out an' then it's very beautiful . . . you can't pay no admission price nowhere to get a sight like that moon shinin' down on the sea . . . .
> JOE: Maybe we can take a walk along the beach later . . . .
> JERRY: Joe, you never know what the women are thinkin'. Now you see, I'll ast my wife what she's thinkin'—ha ha— an' you'll see. What are you thinkin', Mae?
> MAE: An old song was running through my mind. (Singing softly) "I'm the Sheik of Araby, this land belongs to me. At night when you're asleep, into your tent I'll creep. . . ." Anyone remember that song?
> PEGGY: I remember . . . it came out the year I was confirmed. Sister Matilda told the children not to sing it . . . .
> JERRY: Golly, that's a memory an' a half, ain't it Joe?
> JOE: (Quietly) Yes, it is . . . .
> JERRY: (After a pause) I was thinkin' of the stars an' how far away they are, an' that you feel pretty small in the world by comparison. Even when you're dead, the stars go on.

Although there is some slight foreshadowing in the Sheik of Araby line, no details of importance to the play are presented in this passage. Odets is not concerned with formal exposition here, but instead wants to concentrate initially on mood. The lethargy of the opening scene is followed by a gradual quickening of the pace, accelerating throughout the play until the hectic violence of the last two scenes.

Two of the minor figures in *Clash By Night* are especially well-drawn. One is Jerry's aged father, an immigrant artisan who pretends to read the newspaper because he fears he will be deported if immigration officials learn that he is illiterate. Old Wilenski contributes to the mood of the play with his concertina on which he plays melancholy old-country tunes for background music: "It's a Polish song, about the little old house, where you wanna go back, but you can't find out where it is no more, the house...." (I, i).

Another minor character arouses more interest than the central figures. He is Vincent Kress, Jerry's uncle, a despicable little person who sponges drinks or money where he can and stirs up discord as a hobby. Uncle Vince is unquestionably a fascinating villain; however, Odets is not satisfied to make Vince simply a nasty little busybody. Instead he gives the character an added dimension which very nearly dominates the play. Vince is a home-grown fascist, a mouther of glib anti-Semitic phrases and a devoted follower of Father Coughlin: "I'm for reverence, truth an' loyalty. . . . In the new order of things we'd string his kind up on trees! A great man said it, social justice for all" (II, i). Goading Jerry on to commit murder, Vince reveals himself clearly: "The whip! Don't the world belong to the strong? . . . You're twice his size. I'm only half his size an' I wouldn't have it! With my hands—like this—he'd struggle in my hands—no mercy!—no, no! Then throw him off to one side for the rats to nibble on!" (II, ii). The Wilenskis' young friends, Joe and Peg, see Vince clearly for what he is, but Joe's warning appeal to Jerry to cast off his uncle's influence comes too late to prevent the disaster. Joe confronts Jerry with the evident truth about what Vince is trying to do; he even calls Vince "a dangerously ignorant man" to his face (II, ii). But by this point in his life, Jerry has lost any will power he once possessed and has placed himself completely within his uncle's power. His mind vaguely set on killing Earl, Jerry reverts to childhood:

> We had those Christmas cards when I was a boy—a little warm house in the snow, yellow lights in the windows . . . remember? It was wonnerful . . . a place where they told you what to do, like in school. . . . You didn't have to have no brains—he told you what to do. (Beginning to cry) I wished it was like on the Christmas cards again, so nice an' warm, a wonnerful home. . . . No, I wished I never grew up now! (II, ii)

Thus Jerry, in a chaotic state because of his wife's infidelity and his uncle's evil prodding, pathetically blends his father's mournful song with his own childish wish to give up decisions. The dictator is successful when the simple man turns over the decision-making apparatus to him; so goes Odets' allegory. Uncle Vince, Odets' vehicle for all of these totalitarian overtones, is a well-conceived character, though his relevance to the drama may be questioned.

Even in this, probably his most pessimistic play, Odets seeks to temper the despair by the introduction of the young couple, Peg and Joe. Presumably untouched by the sordidness that surrounds them, these two will remake the world. Odets allows Joe the bravura speech of the play, the one which combines his message about fascism with another typical affirmation:

> Am I blue? Did you ask me if I'm blue? Sure, sometimes. Because I see what happens when we wait for Paradise. Tricky Otto comes along, with a forelock and a mustache. Then he tells them why they're blue. "You've been wronged," he says. "They done you dirt. Now come along with me. Take orders, park your brains, don't think, don't

> worry; poppa tucks you in at night!" . . . And where does
> that end? In violence, destruction, cripples by the carload!
> But is that the end for us? No, sweetheart, not while a brain
> burns in my head. And not because we're better than them.
> But because we know the facts—the anti-picnic facts. Because
> we know that Paradise begins in responsibility. And because
> we have the will to see, the honest will to learn! Yes, Peg,
> it's a time to learn, a time to begin—it's time to love and
> face the future! (II, ii)

In spite of this attempt to balance the bitterness of the
drama, the play's final note is the burst of violence that
solves nothing. Among Odets' plays, *Clash by Night* is a
fairly simple melodramatic triangle play ending on an un-
characteristic note of pessimism.

Clash By Night received an almost unanimous bad
press. The attitude of even the friendliest critics was now
one of distress, expressed best by John O'Hara in *Newsweek*:

> All critics, amateur and pro, have had their say at one time
> or another about the sensitive, brooding, strong talent that
> is Clifford Odets. Indeed, Mr. Odets himself once wrote
> for the *Herald Tribune* a critical appreciation in which he
> came off a not very bad second to Anton Chekhov. That
> was permissible. It infuriated his detractors, and it didn't
> disturb us his friends and admirers, especially those of us
> who are aware of Odets' high estimate of his own crafts-
> manship. Now, however, the time has come for Mr. Odets
> to re-examine his artistic conscience and to approach the
> subject in an attitude slightly less prejudiced in his own
> favor. In fact I recommend that his attitude be downright
> unfriendly, in the hope that we will not have another
> *Clash By Night*. (Jan. 12, 1942)

Perhaps in response to this well-intentioned advice, Odets
soon gave up Broadway and began the re-examination
called for.

The United States entered the war while *Clash By*

Night was in rehearsal. In 1942 Odets made one further effort on Broadway, the adaptation of Simonov's *The Russian People*. It, too, was damned by the critics. As a result, he needed rest in order to allow the wounds to heal, wounds opened up by the severe treatment dealt out to *Rocket to the Moon, Night Music, Clash By Night,* and the adaptation. Even more painful was a new sense of isolation brought on by the breakup of his first marriage, the dissolution of the Group, and his estrangement from Clurman. Odets retreated once again to Hollywood.

Chapter 4

THE POST-WAR PLAYS: IN MATURITY
i *The Big Knife*

*M*ORE THAN SEVEN years elapsed between the productions of *Clash By Night* and *The Big Knife*, seven years which Odets spent working on films and, apparently, becoming increasingly disenchanted with the Hollywood routine. In his first postwar play, Odets pictures Hollywood as warped and dishonest. The play includes some highly melodramatic and exciting moments, but it exhibits a minimum of progress by the dramatist. Most of the reviewers took the line of least resistance in damning *The Big Knife*, pointing mocking fingers at a playwright who was now, they said, biting the hand that had fed him amply for many years. A typical review in the *Daily Mirror* read, "After spending seven years in Hollywood turning out movie scripts at fancy wages, Clifford Odets has returned to Broadway to belabor the source of his handsome income." Calling Odets in his review "unrealistic" and "ungrateful," John Mason Brown even pursued the point to its illogical extreme, a fervent defense of Hollywood.

Apparently anticipating the trend of the criticism even before the play opened, Odets tried to universalize the theme of the play. Shortly before the Broadway opening

65

he made some interesting, if somewhat strained remarks to an interviewer:

> This is an objective play about thousands of people, I don't care what industry they're in. . . . I have nothing against Hollywood per se. . . . The big knife is that force which seeks to cut people off in their best flower. The play may be about the struggle of a gifted actor to retain his integrity against the combination of inner and outer corruptions which assail him, but this struggle can be found in the lives of countless people who are not on the wealthy level of a movie star.

This advance apologia did little to convince the reviewers, although the powers of the film industry apparently concurred with Odets; shrewd enough to recognize this script more as a workable melodrama than an indictment, Hollywood quickly turned the play into a successful film.

The Big Knife concerns Charlie Castle, a very popular movie actor who is now interested in leaving Hollywood and returning to the New York stage. But even though his own wishes and the support of his wife make Charlie's decision seem simple enough to carry out, Odets introduces a number of complications. Charlie killed a child in a hit-and-run accident. A minor studio flunky was nominated to take the blame for him, and now the studio has a solid piece of blackmail material for use in holding Charlie in Hollywood against his wishes. The corruption of the actor stemming from this incident is even further complicated by the fact—unknown even to Charlie's wife—that he was not alone in the car when the accident occurred. A young starlet was along for the ride, and now this girl likes to talk about the incident whenever she has a few drinks. Therefore Charlie, having quite consciously made his bed, is faced with the necessity of continuing to lie there by placating both the young actress and his studio boss, Marcus Hoff.

The credibility of the plot conflict is strained by a number of facts. While Odets' Hollywood is a place easy to detest, Charlie's supposedly horrible alternative to following his own desire to return to the stage is a fourteen-year contract with Hoff which will net the actor over three million dollars. The contract even includes a provision allowing the actor complete rights of approval on any script. More important in detracting from his case is the fact that Charlie is not a very noble person or even a very likeable one. He has his moments of sincerity, but the reader must take the word of Charlie's wife or his agent for most of the good qualities that Odets keeps insisting that his hero possesses. More often than not, Charlie appears as a philanderer and a willing victim of decay. He has joined the producer's team in preference to fighting it; he has almost accepted Hoff's attitude that since depravity is inevitable, one might just as well enjoy it. His cynicism is shown early in the play as he is being interviewed by a columnist:

PATTY: The first time we met, all you'd talk about was FDR.
CHARLIE: I believed in FDR.
PATTY: I *still* need an angle for my Sunday piece . . . what do you believe in now?
CHARLIE: What we had for lunch—roast beef, rare!

This cynical mask, the view of Charlie generally on display, does nothing to endear him to the reader.

Once the reader admits the basic premise that a Hollywood producer considers his actors as "properties" rather than as people, the rest of what happens in *The Big Knife* follows logically. This particular producer, Marcus Hoff, is an old-fashioned brigand who uses brigand's methods of blackmail or even murder to keep his property under control. The characterization of Hoff helps the play immeasurably; he is one of the most unctuous rogues placed on the stage in modern drama. A conscious actor capable of standing off to one side and watching himself perform, a character greatly enhanced by Odets' sharp ear for speech patterns, Hoff is a carefully drawn villain:

> Pardon me closing my eyes—it helps me see better. (Pausing) I see a raw youth, but full of that special vitality of talent. And I said, if memory serves, "Son, you're gonna be one of the biggest stars in this business," I says. "And as sure as God made the green earth, you're gonna run into many problems." (He opens his eyes and stares blandly at Charlie, occasionally turning to the others for emphasis) "That's what I'm here for," I says. "This business can run itself. They don't need Marcus Hoff until the problems start. But that's the time," I says, "when I show them why I earn my salaries. And I'm here for you, Charlie Castle. My advice is always free, given with pleasure. I can't *always* help," I says, "but probably *more* than not." And you came to me Charlie Castle, more times than one. Is that true? (I)

But Hoff alone cannot save the play from its normal level of frenzied melodrama.

At this point in Odets' career, some critics, notably Clurman and Brown, went beyond mere carping at the play to express almost psychoanalytical concern about the author. Although no longer a close friend of Odets by this time, Clurman was still inclined to be gentle with his faults. Writing in *The New Republic*, he showed clearly that he was perturbed by the excesses of *The Big Knife*:

> The lack of coordination between plot and theme in *The Big Knife* arises from emotional confusion in the author. It may be possible to write a clear play from a confused source, if one is honest about what actually motivates one's characters. Odets never tells the truth about Charlie Castle, which is that he *loves* Hollywood with a vicious zest, and Odets thinks this love sinful. The conflict between appetite—reinforced by society's encouragement of it—and the insistent cry of conscience creates self-loathing and conceit. The

self-loathing stems from a desire to punish oneself for one's sin, the conceit from an exalted sense of one's superiority in recognizing the sin and wishing to punish oneself for it. (March 14, 1949)

Clurman's facile Freudianism was only slightly moderated by John Mason Brown, who was similarly disturbed by what he thought was happening to a man of great talent:

> It is a silly, overwritten, and turbulent affair. Yet it is not without its interest. Again and again flashes of the old, the welcome, the exceptional Odets talent shine out. In spite of the inadequacy of his story and his characters, there is a communicated, almost frightening sense of Mr. Odets' own unhappiness. Few scripts have made me more uncomfortably aware of the inner despair of the authors; few have left me more apprehensive about their writers' immediate future. (*Still Seeing Things*, p. 224)

It is the cynical bitterness carrying over from *Clash By Night* which bothered Brown and which is certainly the most distressing quality of *The Big Knife*. The unhappiness of the central figure spills over near the end in his conversation with a friend who has just completed a novel:

> CHARLIE: When I came home from Germany . . . I saw most of the war dead were here, not in Africa and Italy. And Roosevelt was dead . . . and the war was only last week's snowball fight . . . and we plunged ourselves, all of us, into the noble work of making the buck reproduce itself! Oh, those luscious salmon eggs of life!
> HANK: If you feel that deeply . . .
> CHARLIE: Get out of here? Does the man in your book get out of here? Where does he go? What, pray tell, does he do? (Bitterly) Become a union organizer? Well, what does he do?
> HANK: Charlie . . . I can't invent last-act curtains for a world that doesn't have one.

The reference to the union organizer makes this passage a poignant comment from Odets on the ending of *Golden*

Boy, when Frank Bonaparte (who is one) remains to state the affirmation after his brother's death. Nothing follows in the wake of Charlie's death. Charlie's suicide seems intended as a rebellion, a final act of triumph over Marcus Hoff. But suicide is an unsatisfactory means of triumph unless it is accompanied by some more positive affirmation of truth, some meaningful insight. For Charlie's death, the only accompaniment is his wife's desperate cry for help which ends the play.

ii *The Country Girl*

Having had his say about Hollywood in the angry language of *The Big Knife,* Odets was obviously in a calmer mood when he wrote his next play. Once again the central figures are an actor and his wife, and once again the actor is searching for self satisfaction and meaningful achievement. But in *The Country Girl* Odets avoided the almost hysterical melodramatics and plot complications of *The Big Knife.* The resulting shift in emphasis away from action toward character makes *The Country Girl* a much more satisfying play.

Essentially a three-character drama, *The Country Girl* brings together a fifty-year-old actor, his patient young wife, and a dynamic young director. Frank Elgin, once a star of considerable stature, has descended to the level of alcoholic anonymity. Bernie Dodd, the director, has memories of Frank's greatness, and when the opportunity presents itself, he demands that the producer of a new play give Frank a chance for a comeback: "Someone took a chance one day with an actress named Laurette Taylor . . . and look what she did in her last few years" (I, i). Frank gets his chance, seems to throw it away, but ultimately vindicates Bernie's faith. The road toward restoration of Frank's respectability is a rocky one, and in the process of traveling that road, all three characters gain new insights. "People don't go back to the same life," says Georgie, Frank's wife. "They go above it or below it, but they don't go back." (II, i).

In one of his early and less temperate outbursts, Odets once wrote in a short article in the New York *Times*:

> Excuse us if we insist upon life brought to the stage instead of the stage brought to life! Excuse us if we do not accept the dictum that any deviation from Ibsen and the Pinero form is a deadly sin. Excuse us for not showing the gun in the first act, because it will later be used in the second. Excuse us for our neglect of a thousand tawdry theatre tricks which make primer plays and quick profits. (Dec. 15, 1935)

But by the time he came to write *The Country Girl* Odets was aware that "theatre tricks" are a necessary part of the successful dramatist's craft and that they do not necessarily cheapen a play. Occasionally Odets resorted to recurring formulas: the similarity of his early endings has been noted, and three successive plays, *Golden Boy, Rocket to the Moon,* and *Night Music,* begin in the same way: with a noisy argument. But generally the theatre tricks are employed with variation and with deftness. Odets was constantly "showing his gun in the first act"—the bottle in *The Country Girl,* the insurance policy in *Awake and Sing,* the Deusenberg in *Golden Boy*—for the same reasons that compelled Ibsen to do so in *Hedda Gabler.* Like any good playwright, Odets recognized the increased interest and tension achieved by anticipation.

Nor did Odets shun other conventions of the "well-made" play when they were useful to his purpose. *The Country Girl* has its obligatory scene in the confrontation between Bernie Dodd and Georgie Elgin which brings his realization of her truthfulness (II, ii). This scene culminates in a classic recognition moment as Bernie gazes at Frank Elgin's scarred wrists, and the involved tissue of lies suddenly dissolves. Moreover, like any other dramatist, Odets had to concern himself with exposition, with establishing a sufficient background to make the current action understandable. Sometimes he proceeded slowly, as in *Clash By Night*, content to work on mood first, and very gradually introduced his characters and their past histories. At other times, impatient to get on with the present action, he painted his background abruptly. In *The Country Girl* it comes in a rather unnatural speech in which Bernie Dodd tells the producer something that person already knows. Though the twentieth century drama has done away with the two domestics discussing their master and mistress, the convention of this sort of exposition cannot be easily discarded. Tom Moody in *Golden Boy* uses a telephone as his confidant; Charlie Castle in *The Big Knife* uses a gossip columnist. But even in *The Country Girl*, the most "well-made" of any Odets play, the dramatist is knowledgeable enough to mask the more glaring artifices with other more subtle ones. The false information about Georgie from her lying husband takes in the reader cleverly: Odets permits the reader to believe Frank in early scenes, slowly to recognize him as a veteran liar, and finally to become impatient with Bernie's inability to see through him. The actor's return to the bottle is deftly foreshadowed by the constant references to his alcoholism and by the focus of attention on two bottles of beer (II, iv). When Frank develops his severe cold during rehearsals, the alcoholic cough syrup is credibly introduced. Shaken by poor reviews in Boston, Frank picks a fight with Georgie, who thereupon walks out and leaves him alone. Everything is neatly and very plausibly in place for the climax. Odets keeps a very firm hand on this material at all times.

The Country Girl gave Odets a fine opportunity to display his intimate knowledge of the mechanics of a Broadway production. Similar to the fight noises that accompany

two of the scenes in *Golden Boy* is Odets' facile use of audience noises off stage in the last scene of *The Country Girl*.
The stage manager is shown bustling about hushing people
during a performance. Most important, Odets' acquaintance with Strasberg and his techniques is brought to the
stage in a convincing manner: the director has Frank im-
provise scenes; Frank loses himself in the character he is
playing to such an extent that he actually bruises his young
co-star when he hits her; in another scene, Frank and
Bernie elaborately dissect the character Frank is playing.
Much of the play is concerned with these acting problems:

> FRANK: But I have to like him, Bernie, even when he
>   puts his wife away. Otherwise I can't get inside him.
> BERNIE: Where do you get these kind of feelings from?
> FRANK: I don't know . . . . (He circles a hand around his
>   chest.) But when I get it here, inside—you can't get it
>   technically.
> BERNIE: No, you're not a technical actor. (I, iii)

How much of all this is accurate backstage dialogue is unimportant; Odets manages nicely to sustain the illusion, and
the reader feels that he is getting a realistic glimpse of the
making of a Broadway show.

   Georgie Elgin, the title character and central figure in
one of Odets' more interesting triangles, is a well-drawn
wife compelled to go deeply into her reservoir of patience.
In a reversal of roles that is significant to the characterization, Georgie, who admits that she married her older husband because she was seeking a father, finds that she has
become a mother to him instead. Her marriage has been
one long series of frustrating attempts to keep the wily
Frank from drinking himself out of jobs. Somehow she
has maintained an admirable warmth and loyalty through
it all. Bernie Dodd is somewhat her opposite, gruff, unhappy in life, yet idealistic enough to believe in an actor
who now needs someone to believe in him. But it is this

once important actor, Frank, who is the most detailed portrait. The furtive drinker, the clever liar, the husband afraid of responsibility, the insecure man, the fervent actor still capable of bursts of passion: these are the various sides of the character who best catches the reader's imagination. As Bernie and Georgie war for Frank's soul, it often seems that they are on opposite sides of the room tugging at Frank from two directions. Actually they are both on the same side, with the salvation of Frank's manhood their common goal. In spite of the title, *The Country Girl* becomes Frank's play.

Odets considered *The Country Girl* his least significant work, bracketing it with *Golden Boy* as plays written only for commercial success. And it proved to be not only a financial success but also a critical one. One of Odets' few notable victories in his skirmishes with the critics came following the opening of *The Country Girl,* when John Mason Brown, who had severely berated the playwright on numerous occasions, apologized rather sheepishly: "Since 1935 Mr. Odets has suffered a sadder fate than Trigorin's. Instead of being compared unfavorably with his betters, he has been compared unfavorably with Odets. . . . He was scolded . . . as if the fault were his. When writers who have pleased us by writing well disappoint us by writing badly, their fate is to be treated as if they wrote badly on purpose." (*As They Appear*, pp. 168-169) It is true that the play appears at times slick and contrived. It is true also that there is no message, no social significance. With one eye cocked toward Hollywood, Odets provided *The Country Girl* with a questionable conclusion in which Frank makes his successful comeback despite the numerous pitfalls, and Georgie, facing still another Candida choice, elects to remain with her husband. Yet it is likely that Odets underestimated the merit of *The Country Girl*. Aside from its obvious theatricality, the play also offers some real insights into real people. The scope is more limited than that of any other Odets play, but *The Country Girl* is a superior performance when measured by what it sets out to do.

iii *The Flowering Peach*

In one respect, a return to the colloquial Jewish family in his last play appropriately brought Odets back to his natural starting point. But Odets displayed a side of his talent in *The Flowering Peach* that no critic suspected in the Thirties. The play is a long way from *Waiting for Lefty* and helps underscore the danger of generalizing about authors. A clever modern retelling of the Biblical Noah tale, *The Flowering Peach* exhibits a calm, compromise, even a humility that few expected from the firebrand of 1935.

Critical reaction to *The Flowering Peach* was mixed, but generally not hostile, and the play became one of the most expensive "prestige failures" in many seasons. According to one writer at the time, William Becker in the *Hudson Review*, the play was the choice of the Columbia faculty committee for the Pulitzer Prize, but the trustees overruled this selection and gave the prize to *Cat on a Hot Tin Roof*. This rumor was verified by several persons with first-hand knowledge the week after Odets' death. Among the daily reviewers, Brooks Atkinson of the *Times* was the most impressed:

> Mr. Odets' new play is a beautiful one. His finest, in fact. ... If you listen closely you can probably discover a message of hope for the sullen world of today. But Mr. Odets is not setting himself up as an oracle. He does not pretend to have the magic formula. Contemplating the long history of the race in terms of some disarming people, he is facing the world with respect and humility. *The Flowering Peach* is his testament to the endurance and native wisdom of mankind. (Dec. 29, 1954)

And while other reviewers made invidious comparisons to *The Green Pastures* or carped at Odets' use of low comedy Jewish vaudeville characters, it was Richard Hayes, the critic for *Commonweal*, who singled out the most significant point about *The Flowering Peach*—its calmness and reasonableness:

> How vivifying it is to hear the Jewish idiom transmuted by tact and wit into art; how wonderful, above all, to find in this time of noisy commitments and harassing coercion a serious statement about human life which never says *must* or *should*, never imposes, sets up programs, announces, prescribes—only draws from the neglected well of our common pieties the small, permanent manifestations of tenderness and affection, of pleasure and reverence and a faith rich enough to nourish the seeds of the world. (Feb. 11, 1955)

R. Baird Shuman's evaluation of this play is accurate: "*The Flowering Peach* is Odets' most poetic and most highly imaginative play. The characters are lovable and convincing; the allegory is constantly present, but not intrusive; the humor is light, natural, and pervasive." (*Clifford Odets*, p. 136)

The fact that a story is well known to an audience is no drawback to a fine dramatist; there are enough great plays based on myth and history to make this statement indisputable. When Odets decided to use the Biblical great flood as raw material, he was following the lead of other playwrights who had seen in it viable dramatic material. Genesis provided a few sketchy characters and a rudimentary story. Taking that story at its face value, the miracle cycles of the English middle ages built upon the Noah legend a simple expression of faith in the punishment of iniquity and the reward of virtue. Yet the best of the Noah plays of that era, the Chester "Deluge," added a comic element to the tale with the introduction of Noah's shrewish wife who refuses to leave her friends and has to be forced on the Ark. This domestic comedy tradition was preserved in Marc Connelly's beautiful and highly colloquial play, *The Green Pastures* (1930). Using a rather slender Biblical hint, Connelly further added to the characterization of Noah by making him overly fond of drink. He continued the portrayal of Noah and his wife suggested by the Chester dramatist and continued also the basic tone of uncomplicated faith. But he placed his emphasis on a more modern theme: the transformation of a God of vengeance into a God of mercy.

While Connelly dealt with the Noah story only as a single incident in his play (a fact equally true of the medieval cycles), the French dramatist André Obey used the deluge as the basis for a full-length play. Obey's *Noah* provides the closest parallel to Odets' drama, and Odets' debt to this French play is a considerable one. Written in 1934, twenty years before *The Flowering Peach,* Obey's brilliant play suggests Odets' in many ways: it is modern and idiomatic in its language; anachronisms are numerous; for the first time there is a detailed characterization of the three sons of Noah; Noah's wife is a simple peasant woman; the central conflict is built on the argument about a rudder; most of all, it concludes with an optimistic affirmation speech very much like the final speech of *The Flowering Peach* (complete with the rainbow—a fine curtain scene helpfully suggested by the Bible). Both plays stress in their endings a note of hope, a willingness to begin again after a disaster. Therefore, when Odets began his work on *The Flowering Peach,* he clearly was not ignorant of the tradition of the Noah plays. He freely borrowed elements from all of them, especially domestic comedy from the medieval cycles, dialect humor from *The Green Pastures,* and modern philosophical argument from Obey. But in dealing with well-worn plot materials, the only essential requirement is that the old story be told in a way that is meaningful and vital to the new audience. In *The Flowering Peach* Odets successfully accomplished this objective.

With the basic action not subject to much variation, Odets concentrated on pointing up the lessons to be gained from the Biblical material. The action begins with Noah and his youngest son, Japheth, at extreme positions in their philosophical dispute. Japheth is a rationalist. Asked what he believes in, Japheth answers:

> Those roads down there! The patterns they make! They're not cobwebs, those roads, the work of a foolish spider, to be brushed away by a peevish boy! Those roads were made by men, men crazy not to be alone or apart! Men, crazy to reach others! (v)

His father, on the other hand, is an unbending advocate of total acceptance of God's decrees. The entire conflict is a dramatization of the compromise of their two patterns of belief. The dispute is made concrete in the controversy about a rudder for the ark. To Noah it is inconceivable that God would want or need any human assistance in guiding the fortune of the vessel. "The good Lord steers the ark, not us" (iii). To Japheth it is equally inconceivable to set out on a long voyage in a rudderless ship. Stung by his father's accusation that he has changed recently, Japheth takes up the quarrel:

> JAPHETH: Because I insist upon a rudder? I can't help it —a rudder is vital to the health of the ark. Would you want me to lie?
> NOAH: Sonny, the Supreme Being who elected us—He made me the chairman, didn't He? He'll see I don't fall outta the chair! (iii)

But when Noah retires to his cabin on the ark for a nine-week drunk, it is Japheth and his rudder that save the ship. Noah still pursues the dispute when he returns. "God never said we should steer the ark! Tomorrow first thing you'll take it off!'' (vi). The exasperated Japheth finally gives in and agrees to discard the rudder. At this moment divine intervention appears in the form of a sudden lurch of the ship which almost knocks Noah down. The ark has sprung some severe leaks. With the ark sinking, Noah finally agrees that a little human assistance is not unacceptable to God.

Though heavily outweighed by the sum total of the play, there are several structural flaws which are apparent in *The Fowering Peach*. For example, the playwright devotes an undue amount of space to the matter of the exchange of mates between Ham and Japheth. This subplot is probably included in order to provide a further demonstration of Noah's dogmatism, but it serves only to divert attention from the central issues. Similarly, there are tangential themes, not stressed intentionally by the playwright, but present nonetheless. One is the question of how essential it is to maintain family unity. Another is a secondary argument between Japheth and his father concerning the nature of God. Japheth makes several angry speeches doubting the wisdom of a God who will destroy the world and all its people. Yet this issue is dropped half way through the play and is never resolved. Finally, the matter perhaps most out of tone is an openly suggested contemporary applicability of the ark. Certainly Odets invites this reading in a number of passages. Though atomic age overtones are hardly necessary for the validity of the drama, the play will very likely suggest such questions so long as bomb shelter proponents continue to invoke the name of Noah. But despite all these distractions from the central matters, the play remains a fine one, the sum better than the parts. As Clurman put it, "Some plays possess so much quality that all their faults are absorbed and purified by it. . . . *The Flowering Peach* is such a play." (*Lies Like Truth*, pp. 54-55)

Although these serious questions are important to the play's texture, the great charm of *The Flowering Peach* lies in its good-natured and often touching humor. While there are moments of comedy in all Odets' plays, he was basically a serious and straightforward writer. But *The Flowering Peach* demonstrates that Odets could write comedy well. His range was unexpectedly wide. There is character humor in the dogmatic, patriarchal father, a stock character who is enjoyable nonetheless. There is an abundance of well conceived, tasteful dialect humor as Odets works with the familiar colloquialisms of the immigrant Jewish Americans that he transcribes so well in many of his plays. ("And our sons with their wives, they're such bargains?" "Maybe you'll stop talking and eat a pair of eggs?") There is a brilliant use of satire on Shem and Leah, the big financiers who stealthily hoard manure in their room on the ark so that they can corner the market on briquettes in the new civilization. But beyond all this there is the quiet, warm, bittersweet humor of a flawed saint who attempts to preserve order through tyrannical means but who learns that it is better to do so through love.

As Japheth casts off his youthful rebelliousness, Noah casts off both dogmatism and despotism. With the flood retreating, he looks sadly back over a life of minor successes, a life devoted to reform, a life, in fact, which is made to sound suspiciously close to Odets' own:

> I'm thinkin' back a good many years. My father's father, Methuselah (Ah, a wonder for the world he was!), he knew I was born for something special—what you call a BIG JOB! "Go out, Noah, go out and preach repentance to the world!" Yeh, that was the story! (Sighing) What should I tell you? Evil is a stone wall. . . . I hurt my head a lotta times! (vi)

Is this not Ralph Berger speaking of his grandfather's injunction? Is this not Odets' own nostalgic look at the fading of his missionary zeal? It is a wiser Noah who recites Odets' beautiful affirmation speech at the end:

> No, I won't get off the ark. Forgive me, Sir, excuse me. . . . First a little guarantee, a covenant, and then I'll go. . . . You know what I want, Lord. Just like you guarantee each month, with a woman's blood, that men will be born . . . give such a sign that you won't destroy the world again. . . . Where shall I look? Where? (Anyone who would be watching sees the rainbow in the sky before Noah turns and sees it with an awed clasping of his hands.) Thank you, Lord above, thank you. . . . But what I learned on the trip, dear God, you can't take away from me. To walk in humility, I learned. And listen, even to *myself* . . . and to speak softly, with the voices of consolation. Yes, I hear You, God —Now it's in man's hands to make or destroy the world. . . . I'll tell you a mystery.

Biographical assumptions are dangerous—even for a man like Clurman who knew Odets well. But it is pleasant to imagine that this deeply ingrained optimism, so similar in content to the early Odets plays, yet so different in tone, was an accurate reflection of the playwright's mature temper. Provided that the creative ability remains on a high level, an Odets who "speaks softly, with the voices of consolation" was an agreeable change from the often intemperate, argumentative Odets of two decades earlier. The last speech of his last Broadway play proved a fitting valedictory.

Chapter 5

THE DRAMATIST IN HOLLYWOOD

*S*OON AFTER *The Flowering Peach* closed, Odets settled in California, with all evidence pointing to an indefinite stay. His remarks on this situation in 1961 sounded almost wistful:

> Well, in some ways it would be much better for me [if there were no film industry], because I might have been more productive in the serious aspects of my work instead of the mere craft aspects. So, in some ways it would have been better, in some ways worse, because I have never made a living out of the theatre. I think I might have been better off if there had been no movies to go to. . . . I would have scrounged around this way and that way, gotten out from under this big tent and pitched smaller tents in many a wild and strange terrain. And good would have come out of it, more good than has come out of my present way of life. I'm almost certain of that. (Interview)

Odets' motion picture career can be roughly divided into three periods. The first was 1936-38; the second, 1943-47; and the third, 1955-61. Odets had his name finally attached to only seven produced films, but he estimated the output of those years variously from fifteen or twenty scripts to "dozens." The disparity is explained by the Hollywood practice of script-doctoring. In his most specific statement

83

on the matter, Odets told an interviewer for the *Times* (Aug. 27, 1944) that though he had written many scripts, he had taken credit only for *The General Died at Dawn*. " 'The others were rewritten for me, after I left town, by four or five hacks to each script,' he says, 'and rather than share credit for what they churned out between gin-rummy games, I decided to pass up fame and keep my self-respect.' "

The seven film scripts that bear his name (with dates of New York release) are:

1. *The General Died at Dawn*, Paramount, 1936. Adapted from a novel by Charles G. Booth.
2. *None but the Lonely Heart*, RKO, 1944. Adapted from a novel by Richard Llewellyn.
3. *Deadline at Dawn*, RKO, 1946. Adapted from a novel by William Irish.
4. *Humoresque*, Warner Brothers, 1946. Adapted from a novel by Fannie Hurst.
5. *The Sweet Smell of Success*, United Artists, 1957. Adapted from a short story by Ernest Lehman.
6. *The Story on Page One*, 20th Century Fox, 1960.
7. *Wild in the Country*, 20th Century Fox, 1961. Adapted from a novel by J. R. Salamanca.

Odets also directed two of these films, *None But the Lonely Heart* and *The Story on Page One*. Four of Odets' own plays found their way onto the screen: *Golden Boy* in 1939, *Clash By Night* in 1952, *The Country Girl* in 1954, and *The Big Knife* in 1955; however, Odets did not participate in the filming of any of them. It is common knowledge in Hollywood that among the films which Odets had a hand in without final credit were *Rhapsody in Blue* (a Gershwin biography), and a controversial treatment of the Spanish Civil War, *Blockade*. (1938). The script for

Blockade in the Academy of Motion Picture Arts Library
in Beverly Hills shows Odets and John Howard Lawson as
co-authors; when the picture reached the screen, however,
only Lawson was credited.

While there is no certainty that a Hollywood contract
automatically carries an attached rider demanding a de-
basement of artistic standards, many Broadway people
have treated the idea as axiomatic. Playwright William
Gibson, who has faced the same problem, commented in-
formally on this point. Asked if Odets compromised artistic integrity in some way by working in Hollywood, Gibson generalized in his response:

> He sells time, and that is the only thing which cannot be
> replenished. Whether there is any kind of damage to one's
> standards by working in movies, I do not know. I think
> that we too glibly assume that there is, but I'm not alto-
> gether persuaded that that is a fact. But you cannot write
> a movie and a play at the same time.

The attitude of a great number of theatre people toward
abandonment of Broadway in the mid-Thirties is nicely
summed up in an incident related by Clurman. Describing
a brief visit with ex-Group member Franchot Tone, he
writes:

> In the afternoon we would chat, mostly about the theatre,
> play badminton, swim in the pool, dine, and see a picture
> in the projection-room, right off the pool. It was quite a
> pleasant routine that we followed almost every time we
> visited them. Once, while I lay afloat in the pool, basking
> lazily in the Sunday sun, Franchot observed me with friendly
> malice and remarked: "The life of a prostitute is pretty
> comfortable, isn't it?" (*The Fervent Years*, p. 187)

In fairness to Odets' detractors, it must be admitted that
it was mainly Odets' own frequent idealistic expressions on
the subject of the betterment of mankind that invited the

quizzical looks and open ridicule when he left New York and began to write film scripts. The mixed feelings evidenced by Franchot Tone soon appeared in Odets as well.

During its palmy days, the film industry in the United States was inclined to hire writers at a furious rate. Any author who managed to produce a best-selling novel or a highly successful play soon found Hollywood agents on the telephone attempting to lure him out of the East. Once he succumbed to the lure, he often found himself ensconced in a neat office, with a dictaphone, a secretary, and some sharp pencils, but with rather little to do.

So it was that Odets, suddenly a famous young writer in the spring of 1935, received his first tentative overtures from the film world. Within a year, his reputation only slightly damaged by the poor reception of *Paradise Lost*, he was working for Paramount Studios at $2500 per week and apparently enjoying the sudden change in atmosphere immensely. An interviewer for the New York *Times* (May 3, 1936) captured some early impressions:

> Some of his friends have spoken with feeling about his desertion of the cause for Hollywood gold. "They call me a rat," he says. But he rather enjoys the situation and is militant in his declaration that the movies will never "get" him. He laughs about his $2500 salary and refers to it as one of the contradictions of capitalism.

The same interview records his earliest rationalization of the process: "If every playwright could spend two or three months in Hollywood each year, he would make enough to go back home and write the kind of plays he wants to write."

But for Odets the addiction to making money persisted, and his frequent and rapid changes of attitude puzzled his admirers. By 1937, Odets had settled on another justification for his continued presence in Hollywood. He claimed to see great potential in the medium which he called "the folk theatre of America." Movies could do much; the size of the potential audiences was a strong appeal to the author who had something worthwhile to say. "Great audiences are waiting now to have their own experinces explained and interpreted for them." (New York *Times*, Nov. 21, 1937) When Odets returned to the West for his second extended stay, during the war, he made another statement which sounded less idealistic: "He sees no more hope for Hollywood than he has ever seen and he still worries about life, art and humanity more than any other five men his size. But he has a steady job now, at plenty per week, so 'Who said I was the man to revolutionize the business, anyway?' " (New York *Times*, Aug. 27, 1944) But, like the hero of *The Big Knife*, Odets could not live with the post-war Hollywood that he saw as completely evil. *The Big Knife* is vivid testimony of the playwright's 1945-50 attitude. Yet by 1955 Odets had returned to the fold, explaining his final move to the West by asserting, "Hollywood has grown considerably over the last few years. . . . American filmmakers are turning more and more to screen subjects of realism and importance." (New York *Times*, Nov. 6, 1955) Deeply committed to the film industry, Odets stated in yet another *Times* interview in 1959, "You can do almost anything you want in Hollywood, providing you're a good writer." (Oct. 1, 1959) Odets' explanations of his stays in Hollywood, each one a little longer, thus moved from the rationalizations that the stay was only temporary, or that movies are a great potential mass medium, to more belligerent defenses of the new Hollywood. When asked about this matter still later, Odets made other revealing comments about his film scripts:

> Let them stand for what they are. They are technically very adept. I have learned a great deal from making and shaping these scripts. . . . It's professional work; I'm a pro-

fessional writer. And I am never ashamed of the professional competence which is in these scripts. I have never downgraded human beings. . . . I've learned to make peace with it [Hollywood]. It seems to tolerate me, and I seem to tolerate it. (Interview)

Yet with or without toleration, the position of a distinguished writer, even in the new Hollywood of independent studios, is precarious.[3] Bernie Dodd in *The Country Girl* probably reflects Odets' basic attitude when he says, "I'm interested in theater, not show business. I could make a fortune in films, but that's show 'biz' to me" (II, ii). Odets must have realized that a playwright tends to become lost in Hollywood. Speaking of the novelist in *The Big Knife*, an astonished Charlie Castle asks Hoff's assistant, "The studio paid him one thousand dollars a week for the last four years, and you can't remember his name or what he wrote?" (III, i). At the same time, there is some merit to R. Baird Shuman's argument that writing for Hollywood sharpened Odets' technique.

Of all his film work, *None but the Lonely Heart* stands as the most artistically satisfying both to Odets and the

[3]Precarious or merely ludicrous. At the time of the filming of *The Story on Page One,* a publicity man at 20th Century Fox put out a release on Odets which, among other things, called him the author of "Looking for Lefty." A passage from this same communique asserted, "Clifford Odets is a theatrical paradox akin to genius. He started out as an actor, then for years ran the Theatre Guild's Group Theatre . . . producing, directing and writing."

During the filming of *Wild in the Country*, there was another release which quoted actress Hope Lange as follows: "I know Mr. Odets is one of the great playwrights of the American theater, but I was not too happy with my dialogue. So I penciled in notes on what I thought I should say. . . . I don't think men really can write good dialogue for women." Miss Lange, so this publicity goes, was thereupon made an honorary member of the Screen Writers' Guild.

critics. In spite of a tendency to play up the more obvious sentiment, Odets infused the script with a sincere compassion for Ernie Mott, his mother, and the other stifled London slum dwellers. Odets' solid theatrical background also helped him in this, his first directing experience. James Agee, then writing for *Nation*, praised the direction highly, adding,

> I base my confidence in him chiefly on the genuine things about his faith in and love for people, which are as urgent and evident here as his sentimentalities; . . . . I was impressed . . . because Odets was more interested in filling his people with life and grace than in explaining them, arguing over them, or using them as boxing-gloves. (*Agee on Film*, p. 128)

In *Humoresque* on the other hand, the sentimentality got the upper hand, though the script was rescued occasionally by a sharp Odets line. The climax of the film is reached in a grand Hollywood cliché. The unsympathetic heroine, rather than continue to ruin the life of the budding young violinist, commits suicide by walking out into the sea, accompanied on the sound track by the crashing chords of Wagner's "Liebestod." While some of the troubles with this script obviously stem from the novel itself (by Fannie Hurst), Odets and Zachary Gold, his collaborator on the project, must share the responsibility.

None of the other Odets films is of more than routine interest, but one of them should be considered in detail along with his plays. *The Story on Page One* is the sole identifiable example of an original Odets film story; furthermore, Odets directed the film. Therefore, this motion picture is unquestionably the purest finished product of any task Odets attempted in Hollywood. The entire work, from its conception as a story idea to its actual filming may safely be credited to Odets.

It is unfortunate, then, that the net result of a tremendous amount of effort on the part of the author-director is not more satisfying. *The Story on Page One* is a rather ordinary courtroom melodrama, not even saved by any suspense in connection with the crime. True to the tradition of the long-lasting "Perry Mason" television series, the defense is clever, vigorous, occasionally taken by surprise by a prosecution maneuver, but never in doubt of ultimate victory; the prosecution team is clearly the villain of the piece. Viewers conditioned by several years of watching the unconquerable Mr. Mason on television would easily forecast the jury's verdict. Odets' script does not even have the merit of saving the unraveling until the end; the viewers are let in on the entire story almost from the beginning.

The adulterous love affair that leads to the husband's death is thin plot material. The characters involved in it are hardly engrossing: Mike Morris, a crass, unfeeling detective; Jo, his attractive wife; Larry, a vacuous mother-dominated accountant. The theme, at least from the viewpoint of the central character, would seem to be that adultery is acceptable, given the proper set of circumstances.

There is considerable similarity between the central incidents of this film and Odets' 1941 play, *Clash By Night*. Both involve an adulterous triangle, a sensitive woman tied to a dull or stifling marriage (with a child to complicate the feasibility of divorce), and a climactic act of violence. However, in *Clash By Night* the husband's murder of the lover ends the play, while in *The Story on Page One* the husband's accidental death only raises the curtain on the area of main interest, the courtroom.

In *Clash By Night* also the waters are somewhat muddied by the nascent fascist, Uncle Vince, who assumes a greater importance to the play than he warrants. Here, too, in Odets' film script for *The Story on Page One*, there appears to be an unnatural degree of emphasis on a secondary character, the domineering mother of Larry. Mrs. Ellis is well-drawn, but the use of the silver cord to explain so many of Larry's problems—up to and including his preposterous actions on the night of the shooting of Jo's husband—is rather difficult to accept. The entire defense case seems to be based on the mother's vicious character.

It is safe to assume that Odets, recognizing all of these weaknesses, wanted his emphasis on another facet of the film, a typical social protest problem—equal justice. Early in the screen play, the young defense attorney, approached by Mrs. Brown to defend her daughter in court, makes a ringing speech about the inequality of justice. He explains to the mother that the state is willing to commit unlimited resources to gain a conviction, while poor Mrs. Brown can't afford even a single trained investigator. Oddly, though, this is the last the audience hears of this theme. With echoes of Zola rushing to the aid of Dreyfus, Vic Santini takes the case; from that point on, the state, with all its trained experts and unlimited bankroll, does not stand a chance for conviction.

In spite of such disheartening drawbacks, there is a great deal to admire in *The Story on Page One*. Odets wisely places nearly three quarters of the action in the courtroom, and, as has been demonstrated by the large number of successful plays with such scenes, there is an inherent, almost automatic fascination in the situation. The dramatic vitality of courtroom scenes is founded on the realization that pretense is stripped away, the antagonists are clearly drawn, and the chips often fall where least expected. So it is with *The Story on Page One*. Vic Santini for the defense and Phil Stanley for the state are cunning, ruthless, worthy opponents. Though the necessity of making Stanley the heavy tends to cause Odets to exaggerate his disagreeable side, he is, nonetheless, a brilliantly drawn courtroom tiger. Aided by some well-drawn minor characters, its vigorous dialogue, and its frequent moments of veracity, *The Story on Page One*, though a long way from the best of Odets' plays, is a workmanlike script.

Seeking a new outlet for his talent and his energy, Odets began a final and very brief phase of his career early in 1963. Even while working on a libretto for a musical adaptation of *Golden Boy*,[4] Odets allied himself with actor Richard Boone and in a flurry of new publicity began preparations for a new television series for the fall. In his last byline, Odets provided a typically flamboyant and exuberant account of how he became editor in chief for The Richard Boone Show:

> To begin with, Jean [Renoir] said one night, over a poignantly delicate bottle of 1953 Chateau Lascombes: "TV, I don't think you understand, my dear Cliff, is, for a writer of your popular inclination, the medium of the future. It is fast, to the point, without frills, wide open for any technical innovations; and the audience is always waiting for you with open arms!" He had made a provocative point.
>
> Only some few weeks later I found myself sitting (sans wine) with Dick Boone, a kindly, bluff acting man, who can

[4]In the fall of 1962, Odets wrote to me about some of the problems he was encountering in transforming *Golden Boy* into a musical. Of course, since the play was being written for Sammy Davis, Jr., there was the added element of the interracial relationships. But Odets was proceeding in his customary exhuberant manner even though musicals were a totally new form for him. He claimed to be finding the experience enjoyable. With a script thoroughly reworked after Odets' death by his friend William Gibson, the musical finally reached Broadway in the fall of 1964 and had a long, successful run. Gibson's introduction to the paperback edition of the musical version is a touching tribute to Odets.

be fearfully direct when rough-house or persuasion are needed. (Incidentally, Dick often reminds me of John Steinbeck, another friend; they seem cut exactly from the same textured tweed.)

Dick was talking about doing a television show together and I was playing the reluctant bride. It was only when he said, "But I don't think you understand. Don't you realize that together, with a hand-picked company of players, that we probably can make the first real theatre on TV?"—It was only then, according to Dick's later version, that I "jumped over the table!" (Los Angeles *Times*, Aug. 1, 1963)

When this article appeared, Odets was already in Cedars of Lebanon Hospital; he was dead in two weeks.

His work for the new television series excited Odets tremendously. He had an office at M.G.M. Studios, where the programs were taped, and he plunged himself into his work with renewed vitality until his death. Odets completed three scripts, *Big Mitch, The Mafia Man,* and *The Affair.*

Big Mitch, drafted during April 1963 and revised during May, was presented on NBC on December 10, 1963. It was Odets' first and best work for television. Considering the fact that the playwright was working within a totally new framework, with less than an hour to develop his characters and situation, Odets showed many expert touches in this play. Mitch is a fine character, a little like Willy Loman, a little more like O'Casey's Cap'n Boyle. He is not exactly lazy, but he is unwilling easily to demean himself by taking work below his imagined "station."

The plot concerns a genteel, impoverished Californian and his daughter. When Ruth wants to marry her humorless accountant boy friend, Mitch is badly shaken; he had hoped for some sort of wealthy Prince Charming for her.

But Ruth realistically goes off and makes her own life. Sad, lonely, bewildered, and left to his own devices, Mitch makes a staggering gesture: he buys the newlyweds an enormous freezer as a wedding gift and then proceeds to pawn or mortgage everything he owns in order to keep up the payments. Finally he takes a job driving a taxi.

What saves this rather ordinary situation is the conception of the central figure who must, at an advanced age, learn to swallow his pride. For above all, Mitch is proud; the symbol of that self-esteem is the freezer. Odets conceived this "North Star" (the original title of the script) as the central symbol. It proves to be an excellent one for suggesting both Mitch's exaggerated pride and his visionary hope.

The best scenes in *Big Mitch* are reminiscent of Odets' early work in *Awake and Sing*. As Mitch and his little crony from next door sit around the house hopelessly watching afternoon television, the dialogue accurately captures the sterility of their existence. Just as the Berger family members seek an escape from their drudgery in the glamor of films, so Mitch and Happy Felcher gaze with vacant eyes and unthinking admiration on the little screen that brings some magic into their homes. Once Mitch rouses himself to a significant, bitter comment about his own life as he watches an afternoon movie on his television set:

> Movie stars, they come and go. It's styles—cycles. I hope they made hay an' put it away. Because, brother, when you go out of style and don't have it, you are just a whisper in the world.

Hampered by a lack of time in which to give his audience the necessary background for his intriguing central character—all we know is that Mitch's father was once

Mayor of Glendale—Odets nevertheless brings alive a small and poignant situation.

The Mafia Man, presented January 7, 1964, is thinner stuff. Merely an exercise in suspense melodrama, *The Mafia Man* is unlike anything else Odets ever wrote. Even the incredible murder at the end of *Clash By Night* is better conceived and better managed than the two that occur in this script.

The story begins in Italy where an unhappy gangster, Frank Ritchie (born Ricci) is living, having fled the United States some years earlier. We soon learn that his son has recently walked out of West Point, ashamed of his father's past, and now Ritchie will return to America and testify against the Mafia in order to clear the blot on his son's name. As he puts it frequently, he wants to give his son "an attitude to live."

The return plane is detained at Orly and during the wait for repairs, an Interpol man assigned to guard Ritchie is axed to death. Clearly the Mafia has learned of Ritchie's decision to inform and is trying to prevent his return. Ritchie disguises himself as an invalid in a wheel chair and prevails upon a nice young unemployed actress to escort him as his daughter on the rest of the trip. But at the New York airport the criminals have been alerted to await the man in the wheelchair. In a rapid and somewhat preposterous succession of events, an airsick Indian mistakenly gets the wheelchair intended for Frank and also gets two bullets. Ritchie flees the plane to seek a taxi. One of the gangsters spots him and shoots him three times. Nevertheless, Ritchie manages to get into the taxi and go to a hotel bar where he had previously arranged to meet both his son and the young actress. As he drips blood onto the bar floor, he is happy when he observes his son meeting Diane, because now she will give Vincent "an attitude to live."

All of this is pretty far fetched, unmotivated material. The central figure is a rather hackneyed type of gangster who wants to do a good deed for his son and is willing to become patriotic (and bullet-riddled) in order to do it. The success of the play hinges largely on any sympathy which Odets can build for his gangster. However, in spite of the humanizing touches which Odets is—as always—careful to employ, Ritchie remains "a flesh and dope peddlar," a man who has spent his life preying upon humanity rather than living as a part of it. And since we have never met the son, it is a little difficult to become concerned about his future.

Odets' final play for the television series reached the stage of a rough draft. Set in a Maine summer resort and a New York apartment, *The Affair* concerns a difficult marital crisis in the lives of two mixed-up, somewhat neurotic people. George Meyers, a jealous attorney, suspects his wife of having an affair with an artist; she actually is having an affair—but with a different man. When George and Ellie return to New York they have a couple of stormy emotional scenes and reveal that the main problem in their marriage stems from the death of their infant son, Bobby. Ellie had turned to a psychoanalyst at the time, leaving George nothing on which to release his own profound grief. The climactic scene, during which George and Ellie discuss their emotional reaction to the death of their child, shows power and insight even in unpolished draft.

The Affair is similar in many ways to the early Odets play *Rocket to the Moon*, the most noticeable likeness resting with the emotional reaction to the death of a child. The psychological insights displayed in the draft of this drama suggest that, had Odets lived to polish it as he wished, this would have been his finest television script.

On the basis of these three short scripts, each very different from the other, it is difficult to make any general appraisal of Odets' work in this new medium. He entered it as he entered his film work, cheerfully confident that he could reach new and wider audiences. He tended to separate his playwriting from his film and television writing, though he frequently asserted that he was not ashamed of anything he wrote. To the end of his life he was filled with grandiose plans; something big was always in the immediate offing. Much as he wished to outgrow his reputation as the playwright of the Thirties, Odets was never granted more. He was left behind the times. Like his almost pitiful television character, Mitch, Odets watched the world pass him by. Hollywood was never the answer. He became an onlooker rather than a participant. Like Mitch he issued manifestoes concerning what he was going to do tomorrow; like Mitch he faced a terrible prospect: "When you go out of style . . . you are just a whisper in the world."

Chapter 6

STYLE AND INFLUENCES

*I*F CLIFFORD ODETS deserves to be remembered in American drama, his claim rests with the artistic creativity of the entire body of his plays and with the influence he exerted on younger playwrights. It certainly does not lie with any special contribution to the political thinking of the depression decade. Odets is normally characterized as a social protest writer, an angry young man, a militant voice from the Left. Thus, one historian, Leo Gurko, writing about the theatre of the Thirties, described Odets in this manner:

> Odets was the official stage historian of the proletariat and the lower middle class, the darling of the left-wing critics, and the bright hope of the American theatre during the middle 30's. . . . His plays were feverish products of the depression and the New Deal, but embraced aims which the President and his more orthodox followers were far from sharing. (*The Angry Decade*, pp. 180-181)

Such fatuous descriptions, though they have long since outlived their usefulness, have stuck. These oversimplifications have fostered the lingering notion that Clifford Odets said everything he knew in the call to strike at the end of *Waiting for Lefty*. But to dismiss him as simply

99

another protest writer of the Thirties is to ignore a great many of his achievements.

Odets developed his own very characteristic style and in one way or another it is still very much with us. Often it combines naturalistic settings with non-naturalistic language. For lack of a better term, Odets' style might be summed up in the phrase "urban middle-class naturalism."

i. *Theatricality*

There is an effective use of theatrical devices in Odets' plays, owing largely to Odets' own thorough training on the stage. The off-stage sounds in *The Country Girl* and *Golden Boy* have been noted. Similarly, the clever use of audience involvement helps make *Waiting for Lefty* more compelling than might be expected from such a frankly didactic play. Climaxes rarely come without adequate foreshadowing. Properties are planted carefully and often take on some symbolic significance, as does, for example, the telegram that Georgie Elgin tears up at the final curtain of *The Country Girl* to demonstrate her decision to remain with Frank.

His Group Theatre experience was central to Odets' understanding of his craft. The capability of an acting company like the Group is sometimes taken for granted, but Odets recognized how fortunate he was in having this carefully trained unit at his disposal. Throughout his life he insisted on his theatrical rather than his literary orientation. "There are two kinds of playwrights," Odets asserted. "The first is the library writer, the second is the theatre writer. I'm the second. The integrity has to be to the theatre, not the library." (New York *Times*, Dec. 26, 1954) The fact that Odets was involved with this organization, that he was at the right place at the right time with the right acting company and directors, can hardly be overestimated in considering his work.

ii. *Characters*

Characters in Odets' plays are drawn almost exclusively from the middle class. Though the economic range of Odets' gallery extends from the unemployed taxi drivers of *Waiting for Lefty* up through the movie magnate of *The Big Knife*, the appearance of a true proletarian in an Odets play is almost as rare as the appearance of a true blue-blood. Even Carl Tausig and his fellow Communist underground workers in *Till the Day I Die* are intellectuals, and what little can be learned of their earlier life sounds suspiciously bourgeois. At the other extreme, characters like Uncle Morty in *Awake and Sing* or Charlie Castle and Marcus Hoff in *The Big Knife* are rich but middle-class nonetheless; they seem uncomfortable with their riches. Except for these few isolated cases Odets wisely avoided the extremes of wealth and poverty. He left the coal miners and the business leaders, the steel workers as well as the club men to the playwrights who knew them, but within the middle-class milieu that he staked out for his own province, he managed a range wide enough to provide abundant variety.

Frequently, Odets saw his characters in allegorical terms. While this tendency did not especially damage *Golden Boy* or *Paradise Lost*, it was a major reason for the failure of such later plays as *Clash By Night* and *The Big Knife*. For instance, since he abstractly envisioned Charlie Castle as any artist caught in a merciless commercial system, Odets closed his eyes to the rather preposterous dilemma that he was asking his audience to accept.

Reflected in his characters is a feeling that Odets shared with virtually every American playwright of this century: a sense of alienation. This feeling accounts for much of the dramatist's concern with lack of roots, lack of family. Yet despite this similarity, Odets' disorientation differed somewhat from O'Neill's in that it was more sociological than psychological. This difference helps point up an essential part of Odets' outlook. Odets was uncomfortable unless he was dealing in social thesis; O'Neill shunned message. Odets drew his characters to life-like scale; O'Neill filled his plays with characters larger than life. Odets generally wrote of the little incidents of daily life; O'Neill dabbled in questions of fate and human destiny. Most of all, while O'Neill looked for answers by probing psychological depths in his characters, Odets continued to look at society. Thus, it appears that a playwright like Tennessee Williams, with his drama of poetry and passion, follows O'Neill closely, while Arthur Miller, with his drama of bourgeois tragedy, follows closer in the Odets tradition. This precarious generalization is not intended to suggest that Odets' characters lack depth; it is only that they tend to remain whole, to avoid the hysteria, the neurotic excesses, and the unbridled schizophrenia of so many of O'Neill's or Williams' people. Characters like Lavinia Mannon, Nina Leeds, and Brutus Jones, or Blanche DuBois, Big Daddy, and Sebastian would find themselves totally out of place in an Odets drama.

iii *Dialogue*

The flavor and pattern of the speech is transcribed very well, particularly when Odets is dealing with the New York Jewish-American dialect. The playwright told an interviewer for the *Times* in 1949:

> It has been implied that the only play I ever wrote out of personal experience was *Awake and Sing.* . . . As a matter of fact, *Awake and Sing* was not a personal experience of mine at all. I never came from such a family, there was never a Yiddish word spoken in my family, I never lived such a life. My mother was a strange and nunlike woman who had to live with two brawling, trigger-tempered men in the house—my father and myself. (Feb. 20, 1949)

But even in the face of such a statement, there is sufficient evidence in his plays that Odets' ear for the cadences of first generation and immigrant New Yorkers—and not exclusively Jewish New Yorkers—was comparable to O'Casey's ear for Irish rhythms. The later plays and television scripts continue the use of such dialogue established in *Awake and Sing*. Nat Danziger, Charlie's agent in *The Big Knife*, inquires, "Where's Marion I can put my arms around her?" (III, ii). Even Georgie Elgin is not immune to the pattern:

BERNIE: Why did he go to pieces?
GEORGIE: It needs an Einstein to tell you that. (II, ii)

There is no better display of Odets' ear for this speech than in *The Flowering Peach*.

The other type of dialogue most characteristic of Odets' style might be termed gangster lyricism. The "tough guys" in Odets' plays can nearly always be counted on to become eloquent at some point, as do Kewpie in *Paradise Lost*, Steve Takis in *Night Music*, Joe Bonaparte in *Golden Boy*, and Ritchie in *The Mafia Man*. Clurman suggests that Odets may have derived this element of his style from John Howard Lawson. Lawson turned to other modes of expression, and Odets took over this style as his own. It soon became his most distinctive trademark, as well as the one most susceptible to parody. (S. J. Perelman's masterpiece on Odets is reprinted in Burling Lowrey's *Twentieth Century Parody*.)

iv Chekhovian Traits

There is a frequent appearance in Odets' plays of qualities which suggest Chekhov. These suggestions derive from the seeming plotlessness, the oblique responses which mark the dialogue, the facile blend of naturalistic detail with symbol and allegory, and the combination of the serious and the comic observation of ordinary people pursuing their ordinary daily routines. These characteristics have, in turn, had their effect on the dramatists who followed Odets. Specific examples of Odets' use of Chekhovian traits have been noted in the earlier discussion of *Paradise Lost*, where they are most pronounced, but the Chekhovian influence on Odets is by no means confined to his early efforts. Gassner aptly described Chekhov's technique as "drama of attrition," a term which fits some of Odets' plays equally well.

In the face of early statements by Odets and his associates which sought to deny a debt to Chekhov, Stark Young, both a drama critic and an eminent Chekhov scholar, replied:

> Mr. Odets' likeness to Chekhov lies, first, in his use of the method of the seemingly irrelevant. Speech and emotion follow one on another without any surface connection. The scene is made up of dialogue that now answers itself person to person, now arises, speech by speech, as if from hidden depths, more really relevant because more individual and more penetrating. . . . It can do Mr. Odets no harm to say that his plays could never in the form they are now have existed without Chekhov. (*New Republic*, May 29, 1935)

On the other side of the question, R. B. Shuman, in his full-length book on Odets, dismisses the Chekhovian influence in a single paragraph.

If a playwright can succeed in investing his characters with so much life that they virtually take over their own destinies, he has reached the ultimate theoretical goal of the naturalistic writer; the characters almost appear to take on a life independent of their creator. Unlike Pirandello, Odets did not consciously toy with this concept. Nevertheless, in many of his best scenes (*e.g.*, Act I of *Awake and Sing*, the strike meeting framework of *Waiting for Lefty*), he achieved this effect. But when there is a feeling of heavy-handed manipulation, as in *The Big Knife,* parts of *Golden Boy,* or the last half of *Clash By Night,* the plays suffer. Moments of violence such as the ax murder scene in *The Mafia Man* seem as out of place and unnatural in Odets as they would in Chekhov. Among other things, Odets learned from Chekhov that violence can be highly effective when it is understated, as it is in such moments as Bessie Berger's smashing of her father's Caruso records.

v *Influences*

The foregoing summary of the main elements of a playwright's style is relatively meaningless if it remains isolated from the movements in American drama. One yardstick for the measurement of an artist's achievement is his influence on those who follow him; clearly there are areas in which the American drama shows signs of indebtedness to Clifford Odets.

What Odets brought to the stage was a very different matter from the kind of American naturalism associated earlier in this century with David Belasco. While Belasco concentrated on fidelity to life in his scenic effects, he consciously superimposed these effects on a sensational and often incredible plot. But the serious playwrights of the Twenties and Thirties replaced Belasco's romantic naturalism with a new sociological naturalism. Odets was among those who helped drive Belascoism from the American stage to its more fertile ground in Hollywood.

Odets' influence on the direction of American drama, while not comparable to that of O'Neill, is nevertheless significant. Walter Kerr, reviewing the revival of an Odets play in 1951, was prompted to suggest: "[*Night Music*] served to remind us that the current—and, I think, hopeful —tendency toward a more poetic realism is really Mr. Odets' invention, and that both Miller and Williams remain indebted to him." *Commonweal*, April 27, 1951) Other commentators have not been so ready to suggest a direct line of influence from Odets. Williams may owe no specific obligation to Odets for his own poetic imagination, his command of the language, his delicate introspective vision. Nor may Miller be in debt to his predecessor for his own power or his notable ability to dramatize polemic. Still, it is reasonable to assert along with Kerr that both playwrights learned from Odets.

Questioned once on this point, Odets himself sounded rather pensive:

> Well, Arthur has never approached me nor acknowledged the slightest influence from me to him. Nor have several other writers. And I was surprised, in some magazine, maybe *Atlantic* or *Harper's,* to find an article by him in which he mentioned the writers who had meant anything to him, myself and Lillian Hellman. I'm surprised that he made even that acknowledgement.
>
> Our literary people—I don't mean this as accusation—nevertheless our literary people have very bad manners. They don't have the European grace, the European sense of one thing passing on from one decade to another, one generation to another, and acknowledging it, or approaching it with some sense of gratitude or some sense of wanting to tell. So I was astonished when one night Marilyn Monroe said to me, "Gee, I can't tell you what your work meant to Arthur." I said, "What did it mean?" She says, "Well, he's talked to me so many times about it." I said, "Well, he's never said a word to me!"
>
> I, for instance, although I had not been influenced by him, I made several efforts to meet Eugene O'Neill. And I would have gone to him as a younger poet to an older poet. I did it with the Europeans here during the war, when there were so many of them here. I met Thomas Mann in that spirit; I met Franz Werfel in that spirit. (Interview)

Of the playwrights who have come to prominence since

1950, William Gibson and Paddy Chayefsky stand out among those who clearly show the signs of exposure to Odets, primarily in their dialogue. Gibson has acknowledged this debt in an informal comment:

> In the evolvement of what later became known as the Odets dialogue . . . lies another point which I had in mind when I said that Odets was neglected in most estimates of the American theatre. If you take that kind of urban hard-boiled lyricism which characterizes Clifford's plays . . . and inspect the verbal rhythms and idioms of such a diversity of plays as, let us say, *Death of a Salesman, The Tenth Man,* and *Two for the Seesaw,* you'll find that all three of us more recent playwrights owe a profound debt of dialogic idiom to Odets. So that when Arthur Miller writes, "A man is not a bird that comes and goes with the springtime," or Cheyefsky writes, "Go be an old man in the winter," or I could quote any of Gittel's lines from *Two for the Seesaw,* this is Clifford's hand which has come down to a new generation. All of us have learned to *hear* certain things in American speech—I should probably say American big city speech—that no one heard for the purposes of the American theatre before Odets, in precisely the same way that no one saw that shadows were colored before the impressionists.

In addition to this observable influence on the dialogue, there is also a less apparent influence on subject matter. It is not very surprising that middle-class domestic comedy is the plot material of two plays, *Take a Giant Step* and *A Hole in the Head,* written by young playwrights (Louis Peterson, Arnold Schulman) who were members of a brief course in playwriting which Odets conducted in New York in 1951. One of the more unusual avenues opened up by Odets' brand of naturalism is seen in the Negro middle-class family life of Peterson's play and Lorraine Hansberry's later *A Raisin in the Sun.* These two plays strongly suggest a throwback to *Awake and Sing.*

Finally, while his own *Two for the Seesaw* is rather far removed in both content and treatment from anything Odets ever wrote, William Gibson (also a member of that playwriting class) recognized an extremely important part of many playwrights' indebtedness to Odets when he stated: "It was the kind of subject matter that his mind was concerned with in talking about our plays which, I felt, brought me out of a literary concern with earlier centuries, and really an English literary tradition, back to the twentieth century and—for better or worse—a non-literary interest in contemporary American dramatic material."

Although Odets remained throughout his life vitally concerned with such questions as human dignity and the place of the individual in a modern society, he did not contribute anything especially profound to the discussion of great ideas in the Thirties. And although he occasionally sounded to the end of his life as though he were writing "with pen held in a clenched fist" (as John Mason Brown once put it), he managed to submerge this early trait most of the time. The later plays are free of the excesses and overwrought final curtain speeches which mark the earlier plays. Odets' early work exposed him to valid charges of excessive emotionalism. But Odets, while retaining his characteristic richness and strength of dialogue, abandoned this mark of his early style along with the doctrinaire speeches. Shuman's appraisal of Odets' growth is justified: "The later plays mark a redirection of the author's interests, but not a retrogression in his ability as a playwright." (p. 145)

The critics and the commentators were at least partially responsible for the false reputation which surrounded Odets. They tended to hunt for propaganda and radicalism even when it was no longer there; they refused to accept what Odets was writing on its own merits and, instead, generally compared everything he later wrote with his first few plays. Many of these same critics had overrated the early plays in the first place; they then proceeded to flay the author for every alleged failure to live up to the false image, the image that they had created. Though a real Odets style can be discerned by a close reading of all his plays, the picture of a frantic, militant, proletarian author simply does not stand up.

Chapter 7

THEMES AND CONCEPTS

*T*HE DRAMA OF the Left in the Thirties was notorious for its redundancy in themes. Certain ones such as championship of the laboring man, attacks on the evils or decadence of American society, pacifism, cropped up with great regularity until they began to sound to critics and playgoers alike monotonous as a broken record. The more skilled of the serious dramatists were satisfied to deal with one or two of these themes, while many of the others seemed to feel that a play was worth while only if it contained all three subjects. Only a few playwrights, Odets among them, are remembered today among the score of social protest dramatists who were irretrievably ensnared by the trap that should have been apparent.

Excited by the magic concept of proletarianism, a patently more meaningful and useful substitute for the Bohemianism of the preceding decade, these writers continued to work over the same material during the Thirties. To their task they brought a great deal of enthusiasm and a propagandist attitude concerning the purpose of drama. In their eyes the American stage was no longer a place of entertainment but a forum.

In the early part of his career, Odets was among those who could not completely escape the urge to propagandize even when the subject is unrelated to the main current of the play. Often this penchant halts the dramatic action. For instance, the trait shows up in a less than subtle way even in a relatively late play like *Clash By Night,* in which there is a particularly jarring intrusion of the anti-fascist theme which threatens to take over the play. Odets wants the reader to consider the events an allegory of the destruction of a simple, well-meaning individual by totalitarian forces too powerful to resist. But critics were not wrong in considering this aspect of the play to be forced, superimposed on a love-triangle melodrama. Similarly, there is a lull in the forward movement of *None but the Lonely Heart* while Ernie Mott, speaking out of apparent context, lectures his older friend on unemployment and the class struggle.

Particularly in his earliest plays Odets shows this tendency to touch all the social protest bases at once. In *Waiting for Lefty,* for instance, the mention of pacifism seems totally out of place. The poignant and meaningful love sequence is interrupted by Sid's lecture about his younger brother who has joined the Navy:

> Yes sir . . . get up on that ship and fight those bastards who's making the world a lousy place to live in. The Japs, the Turks, the Greeks. Take this gun—kill the slobs like a real hero, he says, a real American. Be a hero! And the guy you're poking at? A real louse, just like you, 'cause they don't let him catch more than a pair of tens, too. On that foreign soil he's a guy like me and Sam, a guy who wants his baby like you and hot sun on his face! (iii)

In *Paradise Lost,* though it is still apart from the main current of the drama, the pacifist theme intrudes itself more gracefully. Pike, reminded of the death of his son in World War I, launches into a violent tirade:

> PIKE: Monkey dust! Gibberish! What do we do when we

hear some old bat outa hell say she is ready to give over every fine boy to be blown to hell in another obscene war?! What do we do?!

LEO: Mr. Pike, I think you better not excite yourself.

PIKE: Idiots out prowling the dynamite dumps by night! One struck match and we all blow to hell!

GUS: Better sit. You're lookin' pale around the gills.

PIKE: Who are we, Mr. Gordon? If we remain silent while they make the next war—who then are we with our silence? Accomplices, Citizen! Let me talk out my heart! Don't stop me! Citizens, they have taken our sons and mangled them to death! (I)

Even in *Paradise Lost,* though, the theme seems to be dragged in the back door. Other playwrights of the period —Sidney Howard in *The Ghost of Yankee Doodle,* George Sklar and Albert Maltz in *Peace on Earth,* and especially Irwin Shaw in *Bury the Dead*—concentrated on the single theme of pacifism and, as a result, wrote more effective anti-war plays.

Odets quickly outgrew the tendency to preach and to intrude forced themes; more important, even his early plays rise above that weakness through their superior craftsmanship. It is a tribute to Odets' integrity as a drama- tist that he constantly strove for newer and more expres- sive insights to advance his themes. This integrity helped Odets to survive the decade that had fostered him and to write at least two excellent plays many years later. *Awake and Sing* assumes its stature among the plays of 1935 not because the others were necessarily poor, but because Odets combined certain truths with effective dramaturgy in a manner that other social protest writers found difficult to accomplish. Economic determinism is there, but so are real people. Marxist stock phrases are much in evidence in all the early plays, but so are rich and accurate colloquialisms. Melodramatic clichés abound in the plotting, but these, too, are outweighed by the great number of honest, natural moments. For Odets was much more than merely "the little Jesus of the proletarian theatre," as one critic called him. His plays remain valid because they deal with universals.

Odets was determined to depict problems of inequality and repressed opportunity in American society. His principal medium for doing so was one often used by American dramatists—the family. Playwrights are fond of working within the milieu of domestic life; in American drama the range extends from the ugly Loman family of *Death of a Salesman* to the Norman Rockwell portraits offered by Eugene O'Neill in *Ah, Wilderness!* Since he was dealing almost exclusively with contemporary domestic dramatic situations, Odets naturally showed various pictures of family life in his plays. These include unsuccessful marriages (Libby and Ben in *Paradise Lost,* Mae and Jerry in *Clash By Night*), strained but workable ones (the Starks in *Rocket to the Moon,* the Elgins in *The Country Girl*), and some older couples, presumably past the point of disputes (the Gordons, the Bergers). The notable and significant omission is a happy marriage among the younger characters. Perhaps Siggie and Anna in *Golden Boy* or Shem and Leah in *The Flowering Peach* come nearest to achieving some reasonable degree of contentment among Odets' younger couples, but they are in their respective plays for comic relief. Perhaps also Joe and Peggy in *Clash By Night* or Steve and Fay in *Night Music* are on their way toward happiness in marriage, but Odets does not depict that part of their lives. The suggested conclusions from the observation of all these couples are hardly very startling: marriage accompanied by economic distress is difficult, and marriage must be founded in compromise. This need for mutual understanding is suggested by the ending of *The Country Girl* and is implied as early as *Rocket to the Moon.*

But it is the family as a social organism (rather than specific marital problems) that most often occupied Odets' attention, and there seemed to be a marked calming in the playwright's attitude on this subject that makes a comparison of his early and late plays interesting. In Odets' early dramas, the family mirrors society and the playwright's emphasis is on rebellion. The process can probably be translated into a single axiom: the individual must liberate himself from the bonds of a repressive family; the people must liberate themselves from the bonds of a repressive society. Odets' basic attitude is not abnormal in a Western culture, where the emphasis has tended more and more toward individual achievement, less and less toward a family-oriented social structure. Still, Odets carries the idea to an extreme that is surprising, especially when viewed in the light of the traditional Jewish pattern of close family ties.

Few ties of love hold the Berger family together. Rather, according to the playwright in his note that precedes the listing of the characters, they are bound together because they "share a fundamental activity: a struggle for life amidst petty conditions." Odets follows this stark reflection with another important one. Describing Bessie he writes, "She knows that when one lives in the jungle one must look out for the wild life." This jungle morality extends to *Paradise Lost* as well, wherein Leo barely thwarts Clara Gordon's plan to save the family by dishonest means. But there is no Leo in the Berger family. This is a matriarchal group, and there is no one of Bessie's stature to check her activities.

Bessie's function seems almost exclusively to be repressive, leading one socially conscious critic, Eleanor Flexner, to assume, "What Odets is also intent on pointing out is that the family, in circumstances of poverty and frustration, necessarily becomes an instrument of unjust coercion, even of unmorality, perpetuating false and outworn social values." (*American Playwrights*, p. 298.) Bessie's interference in Ralph's pitiable love affair is a minor matter; her concurrence in the plan to defraud the insurance company is worse; but her connivance in marrying Hennie to the unsuspecting Sam is a pure act of jungle warfare. The fact that Bessie has many moments of humor and affection, the fact that she acts in what she considers the best interests of the family is insufficient excuse in Odets' eyes. Bessie is not evil; *Awake and Sing* is not *The Silver Cord*. It is her *objective* that is evil. Bessie is trying to preserve an outmoded institution—the family. Her father tells her so in plain language. "Marx said it—abolish such families" (I).

A somewhat similar attitude is seen in other early Odets plays. In *Till the Day I Die* "the cause" is much more important than any feeling of family ties. Carl Tausig must dismiss any ideas of protecting his unfortunate brother when Ernst becomes a menace to the underground movement. Even Ernst's wife must reluctantly vote to isolate him from the other party members. Carl expresses the doctrine at the secret meeting:

> What are we fighting for? I need not answer the question. Yes, it is brother against brother. Many a comrade has found with deep realization that he has no home, no brother—even no mothers or fathers! What must we do here? Is this what you asked me? We must expose this one brother wherever he is met. Whosoever looks in his face is to point the finger. Children will jeer at him in the darkest streets of his life! Yes, the brother, the erstwhile comrade cast out! There is no brother, no family, no deeper mother than the working class. Long live the struggle for true democracy! (vi)

And in *Waiting for Lefty* it is Edna, threatening to leave her husband, who is the spokesman for Odets' thesis that the family as well as the individual is of less importance than the solidarity of the working class.

The family of *Golden Boy* has a more pleasant relationship. Old Bonaparte, not nearly so dominant a character as Bessie Berger, is portrayed rather sympathetically because his wishes for Joe correspond to the reader's. If Joe's rebellion against family lacks the idealism of Ralph Berger's, the rebellion is there nonetheless. Turning his back on his father and his own better nature, Joe looks to his trainer and his manager for new ties: "Now I'm alone. They're all against me—Moody, the girl . . . you're my family now, Tokio—you and Eddie!" (II, iv). But Joe's rebellion is incomplete. After he kills Chocolate in his last fight, and even though he has not seen his family in months, his first reaction is, "What will my father say when he hears I murdered a man?" (III, ii).

The half-realized revolt of the golden boy is partially attributable to the fact that the Bonaparte family is not a repressive one and partially to the fact that Odets' own attitude seemed to be undergoing a moderation. In his plays of the late Thirties, the emphasis was gradually shifting from rebellion to search. Odets shows characters who are seeking something to call a family. Cleo Singer in *Rocket to the Moon* has a horrible home life that she is trying desperately to rise above: "Mom and Gert and two married sisters and their husbands and babies—eight in one apartment! I tell them I want to be a dancer—everybody laughs. I make believe they're not my sisters. They don't know anything—they're washed out, bleached . . . everybody forgets how to dream" (II, i). Earl Pfeiffer in *Clash By Night* is much the same. The search is most pronounced in *Night Music* in which Steve and Fay represent not only their own yearnings but those of every character in the play. Harold Clurman's introduction clearly expresses the central theme:

> The play stems from the basic sentiment that people now-
> adays are affected by a sense of insecurity; they are haunted
> by the fear of impermanence in all their relationships; they
> are fundamentally *homeless*, and, whether or not they know
> it, they are in search of a home, of something real, secure,
> dependable in a slippery, shadowy, noisy and nervous world.
> This search for a home—for security of a truly human sort—
> takes many forms, including the comic.

Hovering in the background of *Night Music* is the repressive family again. Fay's father makes a brief appearance
to demonstrate her very good reasons for escaping Philadelphia. But in the main, Odets pictures an essential
groping for family by characters who are homeless.

Odets moved into his late thirties during World War
III, and the lost youths simultaneously disappeared from
his plays. Beginning with the film *None but the Lonely
Heart*, there is a further noticeable shift away from anti-
family rebellion toward pro-family solidarity. Ernie Mott
is a wanderer like Steve Takis until he learns that his
mother is dying of cancer. He suddenly cements his family
ties and wanders no more. When she is first introduced,
Georgie Elgin has packed and is ready to leave Frank, but
she, too, remains. And in *The Flowering Peach* the emphasis on unity reaches its logical end at the opposite pole from
Awake and Sing. There is a great difference in the Berger
family, where "everybody hates, nobody loves" and the
family of Noah, which has love flowing in all directions.
The unbending patriarch Noah is made to appear somehow less tyrannical than the resourceful matriarch Bessie,
even when he resorts to force to convince Japheth that he
should enter the ark. While it is not the dominant element
of the play, the concept of family unity is frequently underscored. At the end of scene two, Japheth "alone and
horror-struck, stands apart from the family scene" as his
father intones a Sabbath prayer: "Oh, Lord, our God, the

soul is rejoiced in Thee and Thy wonders. Here the family . . . is united to serve You as You asked. Give us strength and truth to serve Thee" (ii). The remainder of the play is partially a chronicle of Japheth's return to the family scene.

This family-oriented society in *The Flowering Peach* with its strong picture of cohesive Jewish family life was partially explained by Odets in an interview in the *Times* prior to the opening of the play:

> I have a favorite aunt and uncle in Philadelphia. This uncle of mine is very voluble, very human. It occurred to me that here was a man of flesh and blood who was the Noah of the play. It's important for me to know how my people speak. I said to myself, wait a minute, Noah had three sons, it was a family life, I know family life. There are children and parents, with ambitions, with disappointments, with anger and love. (Dec. 26, 1954)

It is possible, of course, to read too much into this apparent movement. While it seems obvious on the surface that the playwright's attitude underwent a change from rebellion (*Awake and Sing*) through search (*Night Music*) to cohesiveness (*The Flowering Peach*), Odets denied any conscious change in this direction. He said, on the contrary, that all his plays "deal with homelessness in a certain way. . . . I've always *felt* homeless. I have never felt that I had a home. And if that is centrally true of me, and I know it is, that will necessarily come out in the work." (Interview) Yet it is somehow difficult to reconcile this statement with his remarks before the opening of *The Flowering Peach* and even more with the events of that play.

The other area of most interest to Odets as a socially conscious playwright was the American scene. It is clear from a great number of statements in his plays that Odets believed that each of us has a firm responsibility to work for the general improvement of society. Often this belief is put in very vague terms, as it is in Leo Gordon's vision of the future at the end of *Paradise Lost*. At other times it is slightly more specific, as in Rosenberger's injunction to the young hero and heroine of *Night Music* to "conquer disease and poverty, dirt and ignorance." But this is as close as Odets comes to spelling out a program. The most specific action taken is the call to strike, and even this, of course, is not an end in itself, but only an initial step toward achieving the brave new world. No Odets character is shown joining a Peace Corps; no Faust is present to undertake an irrigation project. The idealistic endings of Odets' plays are not endings at all, but, as the playwright said, are only beginnings:

> Frequently, the simplicity of some of my endings comes from the fact that I did not say at the same time, "This is a beginning; this will give you the right to begin in a clean and simple way." But these things are not ends in themselves. A strike and a better wage is not an end in itself. . . . It will give you the chance, in a democracy, to find your place, to assume your place and be responsible for your growth and continued welfare and happiness in that place. (Interview)

Ralph Berger starts to learn when his grandfather admonishes him to "look on the world, not on yourself so much" (I). And the beginning comes for Ralph when he follows that advice, gives up his self-centered complaining about skates, and obeys his grandfather's command to "go out and fight so life shouldn't be printed on dollar bills" (I). The beginning comes for the strikers when they realize a need to submerge themselves in the greater collective good. The beginning comes for Dr. Ben Stark when he takes a close look at his relationship with his wife. The beginning comes for Leo Gordon when he recognizes the brotherhood of the middle class and the unemployed worker.

More often than not, Odets spoke through his plays as a kind of middle-class conscience. The middle class must, as in *Paradise Lost,* abandon its self delusion, or, as in *Awake and Sing*, educate itself to tell the difference between dollar bills and life. It is intriguing that Odets in his plays—if not in his own life—consistently showed money as tainted or corrupting: Sam Katz embezzled his, Kewpie and Fuseli are petty gangsters, Ritchie is an international hoodlum, Marcus Hoff is an unscrupulous villain, and Charlie Castle and Joe Bonaparte are ruined by wealth. The plight of the middle-class conscience is most clearly suggested in a brief monologue, "I Can't Sleep," which Odets wrote in the spring of 1935. In this sketch Sam Blitzstein, a Russian immigrant now working in New York, opens his troubled conscience to the view of the audience and proceeds to torture himself. Isolated from his own family and even more isolated from humanity, he has— at least in his own mind—betrayed himself by turning his back on those true friends of mankind, the Communists. Now as he returns to give a nickel to a panhandler he has passed up moments before, he cries pitifully for forgiveness and acceptance:

> Yes, my blood is crying out for revenge a whole lifetime! You hear me talking to you these words? Is it plain to you my significance? I don't sleep. Don't look at me. I forgot my working class mother. Like a dog I live. You hear the truth. Don't look at me! You hear me?!
>
> Last week I watched the May Day. Don't look! I hid in the crowd. I watched how the comrades marched with red flags and music. You see where I bit my hand? I went down in the subway. I shouldn't hear the music. Listen, I looked in your face before. I saw the truth. I talk to myself. The blood of the mother and brother is breaking open my head. I hear them cry, "You forgot, you forgot!" They don't let me

> sleep. All night I hear the music of the comrades. Hungry men I hear. All night the broken-hearted children. Look at me—no place to hide, no place to run away. Look in my face, comrade. Look at me, look, look, look!!!

This strident confession and plea are forced upon Blitzstein by his disturbed middle-class conscience.

That conscience is the object of frequent appeals as Odets' characters are constantly enjoined to use whatever resources they possess—violin or printing press—to work for the Utopian paradise which Jacob describes to Ralph in *Awake and Sing*: "From 'L'Africana' . . . a big explorer comes to a new land—'O Paradiso.' From act four this piece. Caruso stands on the ship and looks on a Utopia. You hear? 'Oh paradise! Oh paradise on earth!' " (I). This striving for a better world is an essential underlying part of virtually every Odets play. Even in a non-doctrinaire play like *The Big Knife* there is an unmistakable feeling that America must be freed of the Marcus Hoffs if the middle-class conscience is to be placated.

The evident correlate of a need to improve society is the premise that that society is susceptible of betterment. In this concept is the basis of Odets' optimism. Though the playwright disavowed the label "optimist" ("I would say that I have shown as much of the seamy side of life as any other playwright of the twentieth century"), everything in his plays is tinged with an idealistic belief that mankind is capable of improving its own position. The paradise on earth seen by Caruso the explorer can be achieved—if man is willing to work for it:

> In Odets rebirth is made possible because his characters finally reach the point where they lose their illusion of being able to maintain material and spiritual security by enclosing themselves in shells while the sea roars about them. They regain their free, native will to construct their lives in harmony with the love of "human possibilities." Odets'

later characters, Steve and Fay, are the projections of this undying youth in man which will not be denied. Nor do they stand alone. Rosenberger the detective joins them, suggesting alliance between middle-class ideality and the young activist spirit which will labor to put it into realization. (Slochower, *No Voice is Wholly Lost*, p. 260)

Fay expresses best this indomitable spirit:

The last cricket, the very last. . . . Crickets are my favorite animals in all the world. They're never down in the mouth. All night they make their music. . . . Night music. . . . If they can sing, I can sing. I'm more than them. *We're* more than them. . . . We can sing through any night! (II, iv)

Thus Odets' outlook was basically optimistic. The play with the least social significance and a total absence of propaganda, *The Country Girl*, offers an implied message of hope and regeneration. *Clash By Night*, with all its overtones of despair, has its spokesman for rebirth. Even a bleak acknowledgment of defeat like *The Big Knife* has its rebellion, its non-acceptance of the evil conditions (though suicide is probably a mistaken gesture for expressing it). For, as Clurman wrote in his introduction to *Paradise Lost*, echoing many of the dramatist's own statements, "The end of the play is a prologue." The optimism is present in the last scene of nearly every Odets play, whatever sordidness precedes it, because Odets believed in people and their potentialities.

Closely connected with his idealistic pronouncements on American society are Odets' opinions of the artist's place in that society. In both *Golden Boy* and *The Big Knife* the playwright employed a familiar metaphor, gold and the soul, to express a basic idea obviously close to his heart. On the immediate story level Odets was able to make *Golden Boy* a saleable commodity which provided excitement and entertainment for large numbers of playgoers. At the same time he was able to satisfy his own propensity for dealing in significant themes. For *Golden Boy* was not merely a prize fight story to Odets; it was an allegory or, better, a parable, in which the playwright examined both an individual's relationship to society and his duty to himself. Joe Bonaparte's first sin stems from his betrayal of the individual's debt to the group. "My boy usta coulda be great for all men," says his father (III, iii). Instead, with no grandfather Jacob to lecture him, Joe squanders his life in the sin of self-centeredness. Of course that sin is also shared by the country as a whole. American society, suggests the playwright, has glorified material possessions (Joe's Deusenberg car) and the champion (who may destroy others in order to reach the top) at the expense of the artistic and the creative. For the success worshippers of America, there is no place for the second best, a theme Arthur Miller was to stress even more emphatically in *Death of a Salesman*. Those critics who wished to carp at Odets grasped at the thought that it is incredible to imagine a good violinist becoming a good fighter. But for purposes of sharp dramatic contrast to underscore his theme, Odets was perfectly justified in his choice of symbols. The extremes are exactly what he needed. There may be more plausibility in the story of a successful doctor who gives up his society practice and retreats to the New England woods to do theoretical research, or a stock broker who disappears in the South Pacific to paint murals on the walls of his native hut. But if there is more plausibility, there is also less contemporary social applicability in these situations.

Joe's other sin is in suppressing his own better nature. Within him, Odets' hero has some small gifts that should be developed. When he neglects the development of his artistic gifts in favor of his muscular ones, he is indulging in a self-punishment, a destruction of the human side of his nature. The realization that he has completely destroyed the better side of himself coupled with the loathing of what he has become drives the golden boy to his suicide. The morality play aspect of all this is evident: Everyman-Bonaparte forsakes his duty to do good works for God, sells himself to the Devil in return for some large status symbols, repents too late for salvation. There is no turning back for Joe. Odets would like the reader to identify closely with Joe, for the success of this drama on its allegorical level depends on just such an identification. The choice confronting Joe is everyone's choice.

It is significant that disenchantment among Odets' more militant admirers was evident in the reaction to this combination of allegory and deft commercial theatre. Viewing the "new Odets" with undisguised apprehension, the orthodox Left—with Mary McCarthy in *Partisan Review* in the vanguard—attacked the *Golden Boy* theme mercilessly. From the other side came the equally caustic voice of George Jean Nathan. A critic nearly always hostile to Odets, Nathan saw in *Golden Boy* an allegory of a different sort, a thinly-veiled dramatization of Odets' own career up to 1938:

> In that story you have Odets' own impatience with close study and critical application to his dramatic writings, his desire for money (quickly obtainable in Hollywood), his several plays, facilely contrived, that brought him too soon to be hailed as a White Hope, his damaged dramaturgic hand, his increased befuddlement, and—if not yet by any means his artistic suicide—something that, unless he quickly gets hold of himself, may eventually lead to it. (*Encyclopedia of the Theatre*, pp. 292-293)

In this interpretation, Nathan was perhaps a bit closer to a truth about the playwright than Odets would admit. The *Golden Boy* theme became inseparably tied up with Odets' Hollywood career. If a gifted young artist has a debt to society, if Joe Bonaparte's crime is partially seen in terms of his own failure to separate dollars from life, then Odets' own prostitution of his talent (as his friends saw it) might likewise be fairly viewed in these same terms.

In his later plays and scripts, Odets moved away from socio-political subject matter and toward problems of individual human needs, with no consequent lessening of his intellectual-proletarian attitude. The struggle for escape by Mae in *Clash By Night* or by Ernie Mott in *None But the Lonely Heart* is as meaningful as that of Ralph Berger or the bewildered Gordons. But the more mature Odets came to emphasize right and wrong in individual relationships rather than economic exploitation or class struggle. And the ironic result is that Odets more often achieved his dramatic goal using less obviously didactic or emotionally tinted materials.

Chapter 8

IN FINAL APPRAISAL

*I*T IS EVIDENT that Odets always loved People, in that vague, abstract, idealistic way which makes the Thirties writers of the Left admirable and, at the same time, difficult to understand for the often more cynical and more individualistic succeeding generation. Undoubtedly Odets' contributions to American dramatic literature are, at least in part, the product of that love and of the sensitivity or social consciousness which compelled him to become a writer in the first place. There is little reason to believe that he would have written anything had he not been motivated by the inequities of American society that he observed. As a young playwright Odets once asserted in an article, "I see it every day all over the city, girls and boys were not getting a chance. . . . No special pleading is necessary in a play which says that people should have fuller and richer lives." Throughout his life he maintained the same position. His characters are obliged to burst the bonds that restrict them in their middle-class milieu, to avoid being tied down by family and tradition, to seek their own place in the sun. This concept was repeated often in Odets' works, but with ever-diminishing stridency. Early in his career Odets believed that he had a mission, and, like so many mission-inspired men, he occasionally allowed the cause to obscure the logic of his work.

Modern American drama, as John Gassner observed, is characterized by no dominant style. It is highly eclectic. Odets was among the numerous playwrights who borrowed from here and there for his inspiration and his modes of expression. Odets died believing that he still had much to contribute. He was relatively young; his mind was still fertile. And he often thought about his own place in the history of American drama. Quite naturally he resented being placed in any neat pigeonhole that would seem to suggest to him that he was a dead commodity.

Once he movingly indicated a belief—or at least a hope—that his own great period was yet to come. In a thinly-veiled analogy to his past career and his situation near the end of his life, Odets said:

> I think of a painter, a very gifted painter like Chagall. I always use that as an image. A man who was born what, a poor little Jewish boy in some horrible little village ghetto in Russia, who had in him nightmares and dreams, who out of these things, out of hunger, out of the need for —oh, if he only had a cup of goat's milk, oh, if there was only a chicken in the house, a magical chicken. Out of all these things, he built up a whole dream world, forms, images, symbols. And he became justly world famous for the paintings which used these materials.
>
> Now he *is* world famous; now he is technically an extremely proficient painter. What shall he do? Shall he go into semi-retirement? A Beethoven did. Beethoven had a silent period of seven or eight years in which he wrote only cheap little songs for an Edinboro publisher, the Thompson Company. And then, finally, came his last period of work, which is the *great* Beethoven: the great piano sonatas and the great string quartets, and he was exploring a real *terra incognita*, where no man had ever set foot, where he was off the earth, high like some star, some moon. The music was weird; its sound had never been heard. His friends despaired. He himself wasn't sure. He writes to a publisher and says, "I send you this new quartet. You will find it not as arid as the previous one. Thank God

there is more invention in it, and a little bit cribbed from here and there." He meant including himself, Mozart. This is the last grand Beethoven writing.

But a man like Chagall, a lesser artist, says, "I'm famous for these kind of trademarks—a chicken flying through the air, a woman's breasts showing through her dress full of milk, bouquets, I and my wife levitated in the air. How can I change my forms now? I'm famous for this; I continue to live on this."

And Chagall, I'm sorry to say—or I was told this—went around buying back some of his old paintings so that he could re-copy them. He is not strong enough or richly enough an artist, profound enough an artist, to say, "Let me be patient; new forms must come. I have been functioning now for thirty years or more out of my boyhood dreams and nightmares and horrors and beauties and hungers and yearnings and hopes. But now all of those are accomplished. Who am I now? Where are the new forms of the life I've been leading? The life of a world-famous artist? A man who is not hungry any more for a cup of goat's milk, who doesn't need it, who doesn't *have* to be nourished by a woman's full breasts. Let me wait patiently until the new forms come, the new symbols." But he doesn't. So he never *has* a third period. A second he did have, but he will not have a third. (Interview)

Odets was thus clearly suggesting alternatives as he viewed them for the remainder of his career. In terms of his own analogy, he belongs with Chagall, not with Beethoven.

Harold Clurman once attempted to sum up in a single sentence the essence of Odets' significance in American drama: "We should not forget that his contribution to our theatre does not lie in any intellectual or social position he has taken or may take but in the kindness and intuitive brother-feeling he brings to all the themes he treats." (*Lies Like Truth*, p. 57) While this "intuitive brother-feeling" remained strongly imbedded in his heart and mind, Odets calmed his anger sufficiently to keep the more obvious propaganda in check. The difference between the

Odets of 1935 and the Odets of 1955 was well stated by
John Mason Brown when he suggested that if Odets had
written *The Flowering Peach* twenty years earlier, it would
have ended "with all the passengers on the Ark organizing
a union. But the compassion, the humor, the sense of
wonder, the affection and gentle affirmation which combine
to make *The Flowering Peach* so glowing and pleasant an
experience would have been lacking." (*Saturday Review*,
Jan. 15, 1955)

It is a sign of artistic maturity that Odets' plays gradually came to stress their themes in a quieter, less obvious,
less didactic manner. Some loss of missionary zeal is apparent in the words of a fatigued Noah: "Evil is a stone
wall. I hurt my head a lotta times." Militant social activists
may see in Noah's compromises a "sellout" of the playwright's own beliefs, but this view is unrealistic. The
change—if there is one at all—is only a matter of degree.
The successful wedding of theme and structure which
characterizes *The Flowering Peach* can only be considered
an artistic advancement over the too insistent pounding of
message in *Waiting for Lefty*. And running through all of
Odets' work is his concern for the dignity of the common
man. There was never a dimming of Odets' social ardor,
of his basic optimistic belief in the goodness of people, of
his hopes for a better society. If there is one dominant attitude to be found in all of Odets' works, it is the one which
Charlie Castle claims he learned from reading Victor
Hugo: " 'Love people, do good, help the lost and fallen,
make the world happy, if you can!' "

Bibliography

I. By Odets

Plays:

The Big Knife. New York: Random House, 1949.
Clash By Night. New York: Random House, 1942.
The Country Girl. New York: Viking Press, 1951.
The Flowering Peach. In *The Best Plays of 1954-1955*, ed. Louis Kronenberger. New York: Dodd, Mead, 1955. (condensed)
Night Music. New York: Random House, 1940.
[A Scene from] *The Silent Partner, New Theatre and Film*, IV (March 1937) 5-9.
Six Plays of Clifford Odets. New York: Random House, 1939. (Contains *Waiting for Lefty, Till the Day I Die, Awake and Sing, Paradise Lost, Golden Boy*, and *Rocket to the Moon* as well as a Preface by Odets and Three Introductions by Harold Clurman.)
Waiting for Lefty (original version), *New Theatre*, II (February 1935), 13-20.

Articles:

"Boone, Renoir Find Common Ground," Los Angeles *Times*, Aug. 1, 1963, Sec. IV, p. 16.
"Democratic Vistas in Drama," New York *Times*, Nov. 21, 1937, Sec. XI, pp. 1-2.
"Genesis of a Play," New York *Times*, Feb. 1, 1942, Sec. IX, p. 3.
"How a Playwright Triumphs," (Discussion with Arthur Wagner) *Harper's*, CCXXXIII (September 1966), 64-70.
"In Praise of a Maturing Industry," New York *Times*, Nov. 6, 1955, Sec. II, p. 5.
"On Coming Home," New York *Times*, July 25, 1948, Sec. II, p. 1.
"Some Problems of the Modern Dramatist," New York *Times*, Dec. 15, 1935, Sec. XI, p. 3.
"To Whom It May Concern: Marilyn Monroe," *Show*, II (October 1962), 67, 136.

"The Transient Olympian," *Show*, III (April 1963), 106-107, 130-133.

"Two Approaches to the Writing of a Play," New York *Times*, April 22, 1951, Sec. II, pp. 1-2.

"When Wolfe Came Home," New York *Times*, Sept. 14, 1958, Sec. II, p. 3.

"Willem de Kooning," *The Critic*, XXI (Oct.-Nov. 1962), 37-38.

Miscellany:

Beals, Carleton, and Clifford Odets. "Rifle Rule in Cuba." New York: Provisional Committee for Cuba, 1935.

Humoresque. Unpublished manuscript, 1945.

Big Mitch, The Mafia Man, The Affair. Unpublished manuscripts for The Richard Boone Show, 1963.

"I Can't Sleep," a monologue. *New Theatre*, III (February 1936), 8-9.

"None but the Lonely Heart." In *Best Film Plays, 1945*, ed. John Gassner and Dudley Nichols. New York: Crown, 1946.

The Story on Page One. Unpublished manuscript, 1959.

II. Secondary Sources

Books:

Aaron, Daniel. *Writers on the Left*. New York: Harcourt, Brace, 1961.

Agee, James. *Agee on Film*. New York: McDowell, Obolensky, 1958.

Block, Anita. *The Changing World in Plays and Theatre*. Boston: Little, Brown, 1939.

Brown, John Mason. *As They Appear*. New York: McGraw-Hill, 1952.

——————. *Broadway in Review*. New York: W. W. Norton, 1940.

——————. *Seeing More Things*. New York: McGraw-Hill, 1948.

——————. *Seeing Things*. New York: McGraw-Hill, 1946.

——————. *Still Seeing Things*. New York: McGraw-Hill, 1950.

——————. *Two on the Aisle*. New York: W. W. Norton, 1938.

Clurman, Harold. *The Fervent Years*. New York: Hill and Wang, 1957.

——————. *Lies Like Truth*. New York: Macmillan, 1958.

——————. Three Introductions. *In Six Plays of Clifford Odets*. New York: Random House, 1939.

Downer, Alan S. *Fifty Years of American Drama*. Chicago: Regnery, 1951.

Drew, Elizabeth. *Discovering Drama*. New York: W. W. Norton, 1937.

Dusenberry, Winifred L. *The Theme of Loneliness in Modern American Drama*. Gainesville: University of Florida Press, 1960.

Flexner, Eleanor. *American Playwrights: 1918-1938*. New York: Simon and Schuster, 1938.

Gagey, Edmond M. *Revolution in American Drama*. New York: Columbia University Press, 1947.

Gassner, John. *Masters of the Drama*, 3rd rev. ed. New York: Dover, 1954.

——————. *Theatre at the Crossroads*. New York: Holt, Rinehart and Winston, 1960.

——————. *The Theatre in Our Times*. New York: Crown, 1954.

Gibson, William. Introduction to *Golden Boy* (musical version). New York: Bantam Books, 1966.

Goldstein, Malcolm. "Clifford Odets and the Found Generation." In *American Drama and Its Critics*. Chicago: University of Chicago Press, 1965.

Gorelik, Mordecai. *New Theatres for Old*. New York: Samuel French, 1940.

Griffin, Robert J. "On the Love Songs of Clifford Odets." In *The Thirties*. DeLand, Florida: Everett/Edwards, 1967.

Himelstein, Morgan Y. *Drama Was a Weapon*. New Brunswick, N. J.: Rutgers University Press, 1963.

Hopper, Stanley Romaine, ed. *Spiritual Problems in Contemporary Literature*. New York: Harper and Brothers, 1952.

Kazin, Alfred. *Starting Out in the Thirties*. Boston: Atlantic, Little Brown, 1965.

Krutch, Joseph Wood. *The American Drama Since 1918*. New York: George Braziller, 1957.

Lawson, John Howard. *Theory and Technique of Playwriting and Screenwriting*. New York: G. P. Putnam's Sons, 1949.

Mantle, Burns. *Contemporary American Playwrights*. New York: Dodd, Mead, 1939.

McCarthy, Mary. *Sights and Spectacles*. New York: Farrar, Strauss, 1956.

Mendelsohn, Michael. "Clifford Odets: The Artist's Commitment." In *Literature and Society*. Lincoln: University of Nebraska Press, 1964.

Mersand, Joseph. *The American Drama, 1930-1940*. New York: The Modern Chapbooks, 1941.

Morris, Lloyd. *Postscript to Yesterday*. New York: Random House, 1947.

Murray, Edward. *Clifford Odets*: *The Thirties and After*. New York: Frederick Ungar, 1968.

Nathan, George Jean. *Encyclopaedia of the Theatre*. New York: Alfred A. Knopf, 1940.

O'Hara, Frank H. *Today in American Drama*. Chicago: University of Chicago Press, 1939.

Rabkin, Gerald. *Drama and Commitment*. Bloomington: University of Indiana Press, 1964.

Shuman, R. Baird. *Clifford Odets*. New York: Twayne, 1962.

Slochower, Harry. *No Voice is Wholly Lost*. Toronto: McClelland and Stewart, 1945.

Tynan, Kenneth. *Curtains*. New York: Athenium, 1961.

Periodicals:

Becker, William. "Reflections on Three New Plays," *Hudson Review*, VIII (Summer 1955), 263-268.

Brown, John Mason. "On the Crest of the Waves," *Saturday Review*, XXXVIII (Jan. 15, 1955), 30.

Clurman, Harold. "Around *Night Music*," *New Republic*, CXXIV (April 30, 1951), 22.

——————. "Clifford Odets," *Saturday Review*, XLVI (Sept. 14, 1963), 10.

——————. "The First Fifteen Years," *New Republic*, CXXIII (Dec. 11, 1950), 29-30.

——————. "Sins of Clifford Odets," *New Republic*, CXX (March 14, 1949), 28-29.

"Credo of a Wrong-Living Man," *Time*, LXXX (Dec. 14, 1962), 40.

Fagin, N. B. "In Search of an American *Cherry Orchard*, *Texas Quarterly*, I (Summer-Autumn 1958), 132-141.

Ferguson, Otis. "Pay-off on Odets," *New Republic*, C (Sept. 27 and Oct. 4, 1939), 216-217; 242-243.

Gassner, John. "The Long Journey of a Talent," *Theatre Arts*, XXXIII (July 1949), 24-30.

———————. "Playwrights of the Period," *Theatre Arts*, XLIV (September 1960), 19-22, 69-71.

Gibbs, Wolcott. "The Ring and the Bow," *New Yorker*, XXVIII (March 22, 1952), 54.

Goldstone, Richard H. "The Making of Americans: Clifford Odets' Implicit Theme," Proceedings of the IVth Congress of the International Comparative Literature Association, 1966, 654-660.

Hayes, Richard. "The Flowering Peach," *Commonweal*, LXI (Feb. 11, 1955), 502-503.

Hunt, Albert, "Only Soft-Centred Left," *Encore*, VIII (May-June 1961), 5-12.

Hyams, Barry. "Twenty Years on a Tightrope," *Theatre Arts*, XXXIX (April 1955), 68-70, 86.

Isaacs, Edith J. R. "Clifford Odets, First Chapters," *Theatre Arts*, XXIII (April 1939), 257-264.

Kauffmann, Stanley, "Is Artistic Integrity Enough?" *New Republic*, CXLII (Feb. 8, 1960), 22.

Kerr, Walter. "Night Music," *Commonweal*, LIV (April 27, 1951), 58-59.

McCarten, John. "Revolution's Number One Boy," *New Yorker*, XIII (Jan. 22, 1938), 21-27.

McCarthy, Mary. "Realism in the American Theatre," *Harper's*, CCXXIII (July 1961), 45-52.

Mendelsohn, Michael. "Clifford Odets and the American Family," *Drama Survey*, III (Fall 1963), 238-243.

———————. "Odets at Center Stage: A Talk With Michael J. Mendelsohn," *Theatre Arts*, XLVII (May 1963 and June 1963), 16-19, 74-76; 28-30, 78-80.

Nathan, George Jean. "The White Hope Gets Paler," *Newsweek*, XV (March 4, 1940), 42.

"Odets and the Comrades," *Newsweek*, XXXIX (June 2, 1952), 23.

O'Hara, John. "Desire Under the Rose," *Newsweek*, XIX (Jan. 12, 1942), 46.

Sugrue, Thomas. "Mr. Odets Regrets," *American Magazine*, CXXII (October 1936), 42-43, 106-108.

Vernon, Grenville. "Mr. Odets' Plays Are Jewish," *Commonweal*, XXIX (Dec. 16, 1938), 215.

Warshow, Robert S. "Poet of the Jewish Middle Class," *Commentary*, I (May 1946), 17-22.

"White Hope," *Time*, XXXII (Dec. 5, 1938), 44-47.

Young, Stark, "Awake and Whistle at Least," *New Republic,* LXXXII (March 13, 1935), 134.

————. "Lefty and Nazi," *New Republic,* LXXXII (April 10, 1935), 247.

————. "New Talent," *New Republic,* LXXXIII (May 29, 1935), 78.

Newspaper Articles:

Atkinson, Brooks, "Odets Not a Failure," New York *Times*, Sept. 3, 1963, p. 30.

Berch, Barbara. "Going Their Way Now?" New York *Times*, Aug. 27, 1944, Sec. II, p. 3.

Clurman, Harold. "Clifford Odets' Ideals," New York *Times*, Aug. 25, 1963, Sec. II, p. 1.

"Mr. Odets is Acclimated," New York *Times*, May 3, 1936, Sec. X, p. 4.

Mitgang, Herbert. "Odets Goes to Genesis," New York *Times*, Dec. 26, 1954, Sec. II, p. 1.

Norton, Elliot. "Clifford Odets Sans Message," New York *Times*, Nov. 5, 1950, Sec. II, p. 3.

Peck, Seymour. "An Angry Man from Hollywood," New York *Times*, Feb. 20, 1949, Sec. II, p. 1.

Schumach, Murray. "Hollywood Gets Unusual Praise," New York *Times*, Oct. 1, 1959, p. 39.

Government Document:

House Committee on Un-American Activities, *Hearings*, May 19-21, 1952. "Communist Infiltration of the Hollywood Motion-Picture Industry, Part 8," pp. 3453-3512.

Index

Adler, Luther 18
Adler, Stella 11
Affair, The 93, 96-97
Anderson, Maxwell 9
Awake and Sing xiv, 1, 2, 5, 15, 28-33, 34, 38, 43, 46, 47, 48, 55 56, 71, 94, 101-104, 113, 116, 118, 119, 121, 122

Belasco, David 105
Bellow, Saul xiii
Big Knife, The 3, 17, 18, 65-70, 72, 84, 87, 88, 101, 103, 105, 122, 123
Big Mitch 93-95
Blockade 84-85
Brecht, Bertolt 24
Bromberg, J. Edward 11-12

Carnovsky, Morris 11, 18
Chagall, Marc 128-129
Chayefsky, Paddy xiii, 107
Chekhov, Anton xiv, 4, 33-35, 62, 103-105
Cherry Orchard, The 33-36
Clash By Night 5, 16, 58-63, 65, 69, 72, 84, 90, 95, 101, 105, 112, 114, 117, 123, 126
Clurman, Harold x, xv, 3, 5, 7-16, 21, 38-40, 48, 57-58, 63, 68, 79, 81, 85, 103, 117, 123, 129
Communist Party of the U.S. 11-14
Connelly, Marc 77
Country Girl, The 1, 18, 45, 55, 70-75, 84, 88, 100, 114, 123

Crawford, Cheryl 8-9
Cuba 12-13

Deadline at Dawn 84
Death of a Salesman 37, 107, 114, 124
Dos Passos, John 6

Faulkner, William xvi
Farrell, James T. 6
Fervent Years, The x, xv, 5, 7, 8-12, 39, 41, 48, 85
Flowering Peach, The ix, 1, 18, 26, 75-81, 83, 103, 114, 118-119, 130

General Died at Dawn, The 84
Gibson, Margaret Brenman x, xi, 5
Gibson, William xi, 85, 92, 107-108
Golden Boy 5, 16, 18, 27, 43-47, 48, 55, 69, 71-74, 84, 92, 100, 101, 103, 105, 114, 117, 123-126
Grayson, Bette 17
Green Pastures, The 76-77
Green, Paul 8
Group Theatre xv, 2, 3, 8-16, 53, 63, 100

Hansberry, Lorraine 107
Hellman, Lillian 106
Hemingway, Ernest xvii
Howard, Sidney 113
Hugo, Victor 3, 130
Humoresque 84, 89

"I Can't Sleep" 121-122

James, Henry 19
Juno and the Paycock 32

Kaye, Danny x
Kazan, Elia 10, 18
Kingsley, Sidney 9, 14

Lawson, John Howard xvi, 6, 23, 41-42, 85, 103
Levy, Melvin 14
Llewellyn, Richard 17

Mafia Man, The 93, 95-96, 103, 105
Malamud, Bernard xiii
Maltz, Albert 113
Miller, Arthur xiii, xvii, 37, 102, 106, 124
Monroe, Marilyn 106
Murray, Edward ix-x

Nathan, George Jean 51-52, 54, 125
Night Music 5, 16, 46, 52-58, 63, 71, 103, 105, 114, 117-120, 123
None but the Lonely Heart 17, 84, 88-89, 112, 118, 126

Obey, André 77
O'Casey, Sean xvi, 32-33, 93, 103
O'Neill, Eugene xiii, xvii, 2, 4-5, 101-102, 105-106, 114

Paradise Lost 5, 15, 33-39, 43, 45, 46, 47, 49, 52, 53, 56, 86, 101, 103, 104, 112-115, 120, 121, 123
Peterson, Louis 107

Pirandello, Luigi 24, 41-42, 104
Podhoretz, Norman xiii

Rainer, Luise 16, 41, 48
Rhapsody In Blue 84
Rice, Elmer 54
Richard Boone Show, The 19, 92-97
Rocket to the Moon 16, 40, 47-52, 53, 63, 71, 97, 114, 117
Roth, Philip xiii
Russian People, The 17, 63

Saroyan, William 53-54
Schulman, Arnold 107
Shaw, Irwin 113
Shuman, R. Baird ix, xi, 76, 88, 104, 108
Sifton, Claire and Paul 9
Silent Partner, The 16, 39-41, 43, 52
Sklar, George 113
Stanislavsky, Konstantin 11
Steinbeck, John 6
Story on Page One, The 84, 88, 89-92
Strasberg, Lee 8-11, 16
Sweet Smell of Success, The 84

Till the Day I Die 2, 5, 15, 26-28, 40, 45, 101, 116
Tone, Franchot 85

Waiting for Lefty ix, 1, 2, 9, 15, 21-26, 27-28, 31, 37-38, 40, 53, 75, 99-101, 104, 112, 116, 130
Wexley, John xvi
Wilder, Thornton 24
Wild in the Country 84, 88
Williams, Tennessee 102, 106